PRAISE FOR

THE CREATIVE PENDULUM

"The Creative Pendulum is an exceptional book on dowsing that goes far beyond the basics. Readers are invited to dig deep into the creative and intuitive side of pendulums, exploring practices as diverse as clearing your aura and choosing the best social media platform. Included is an extensive selection of pendulum exercises, thirty-three charts, and details on using pendulums to set up an intuitive coaching practice. In my many years of dowsing, this is the best reference material I've seen."

—NANCY HENDRICKSON, author of *Ancestral Tarot*

"The Creative Pendulum is a masterpiece of soul awakening and creative manifestation. Joan Rose Staffen is an accomplished artist and a healer, and both qualities shine in her new book. While many regard the ancient art of pendulum divination as an externalized practice, Joan demonstrates that pendulum divining is truly a *creative skill*, similar to that of an artist who uses a paintbrush with inner attunement and vision. The vibrant processes and practical life examples outlined in *The Creative Pendulum* show how the soul can truly "paint" its own dynamic landscape of enhanced consciousness, thereby activating one's life with greater purpose, passion, and empowerment."

—PATRICIA KAMINSKI, executive director, Flower Essence Society *www.flowersociety.org*

"If you are a writer or an artist or a poet and have found yourself struggling with blocks to your creativity, you will enjoy every moment of *The Creative Pendulum* by Joan Rose Staffen. Joan Rose guides us through the spiritual and meditative side of our creative life. She connects us with our own insights and gives us tools to use a higher and deeper level of inner guidance. Using Joan Rose's pendulum methods yields a clarity not only to our passions for creativity but also to the act of living."

—CATHERINE SEGURSON, founder and editor-in-chief of *Catamaran Literary Reader*

"A wonderful book that will empower your intuition and help you to tap into your creative nature with the use of a pendulum and charts, *The Creative Pendulum* is full of insightful guidance and knowledge that places you in great creative control of your life path."

—JOANNE BROCAS, bestselling author of *Clear Spirit*

THE CREATIVE PENDULUM

Keys to Unlock Your Innovative Spirit

JOAN ROSE STAFFEN

WEISER BOOKS

*Dedicated to all my wonderful, creative clients
and students who teach me so much!*

This edition first published in 2022 by Weiser Books, an imprint of
Red Wheel/Weiser, LLC

With offices at:
65 Parker Street, Suite 7
Newburyport, MA 01950
www.redwheelweiser.com

ISBN: 978-1-57863-751-5

Library of Congress Cataloging-in-Publication Data available upon request.

Cover design by Kathryn Sky-Peck
Cover art by Shutterstock
Interior by Happenstance Type-O-Rama
Typeset in Alido, New Aster LT Std, Wood Poster Display

Printed in Canada
MAR

10 9   8 7 6 5 4 3 2 1

CONTENTS

Introduction: Opening to the Divine, Creative Self *1*

Chapter 1. Where Divining, Healing, and Creativity Meet 9

Chapter 2. Learn to Dowse with the Pendulum *15*

Chapter 3. Divine with the Intuitive Creativity Charts
(Charts 1–2) 23

Chapter 4. Clear Your Life and Balance Your Aura and
Chakras (Charts 3–4) *31*

Chapter 5. Create Time for Morning Quiet and Inspiration
(Charts 5–6) *40*

Chapter 6. What's Standing in Your Way? Uncover Negative Beliefs,
Blocks, and Distractions, and Find Solutions (Charts 7–10) 48

Chapter 7. Fill the Creative Well (Charts 11–14) *72*

Chapter 8. Discover Your Creative Identity and New
Art Directions (Charts 15–20) *86*

Chapter 9. Use Conscious Creative Processes and Tools
(Charts 21–24) *100*

Chapter 10. Venture into the Business of Art (Charts 25–26) *118*

Chapter 11. Out into the World: Market Your Art (Charts 27–31) *130*

Chapter 12. Action and Success: Why Not? Isn't It Time?
(Charts 32–33) *142*

Chapter 13. Coach Yourself to Personal Success *156*

Chapter 14. Coach Others: Discover Their Gifts and Motivate
Them to Take Action *167*

Chapter 15. Paint on Your Hands: Art Prompts *182*

Chapter 16. Start Your Own Divine Creativity Cluster *198*

Acknowledgments *206*

Bibliography and Recommended Reading *208*

Appendix: The Thirty-Three Intuitive Creativity Charts *212*

THE INTUITIVE CREATIVITY CHARTS

1. Yes/No and Clearing
2. Time and Percent
3. Clearing Needed
4. Aura and Chakras
5. Morning Quiet Time
6. Inspiration
7. Negative Beliefs
8. Distractions
9. Creative Blocks
10. Solutions
11. Artist Needs
12. Play and Learn
13. Spark Creativity
14. Support Team
15. Creative Identity
16. Digital Arts
17. Home Arts
18. Literary Arts
19. Performing Arts
20. Visual Arts
21. Creative Process
22. Principles of Design
23. Color
24. Elements of Story and Writing
25. Business of Art
26. Income Streams
27. Marketing
28. Audience
29. Target Location
30. Sales Venue
31. Social Media
32. Intuitive Action Plan
33. Success

INTRODUCTION

Opening to the Divine, Creative Self

> *There is an underlying, in-dwelling creative force infusing all of life—including ourselves.*
>
> —JULIA CAMERON, *The Artist's Way*

How do you engage your inner creative self? How do you open to that place where time and space seem to disappear and you are alert and focused? A place where you do not strive or strain and you know you are enough? How do you get from ordinary reality to that imaginative, visionary space where you are in tune with the Great Creator?

The Creative Pendulum is a guide to an intuitive coaching system with an art case of intuitive tools. As you uncover buried aspects of your inner gifted self through the many methods discussed, you will discover new interests, aptitudes, and talents that lead to an innovative, rewarding path forward.

By reading *The Creative Pendulum,* you can learn to dowse with a pendulum and use the thirty-three Intuitive Creativity Charts that you will find at the back of this book. With these charts, you will learn to clear your aura and chakras and any negative beliefs and distractions that block your creativity. You'll learn to ask for and receive both mystical and practical solutions and guidance, and align with Spirit. You'll be able to coach yourself and others while using the Intuitive Creativity Coaching forms and the Intuitive Action Plan. You will also find a wealth of ideas, art-making exercises, and stories to inspire and encourage you.

Yet, as you read, an inner voice might instantly arise: "Who am I to be creative? How can I be creative? I've never thought of myself as artistic." But you can reply to the skeptic within by saying, "I am. I am a child/an adult of the Great Creator that gave birth to the infinite universe, the sun and planets, and all the trees, plants, animals, birds, and *me*. And I am curious."

The Process of Pendulum Creativity

You will learn the following process step-by-step throughout the book. You will be amazed at your newfound abilities and progress.

- Attune to and commune with Spirit through centering and meditation.
- Learn to dowse (also called divining) with a pendulum.
- Research using the pendulum with the Intuitive Creativity Charts.
- Let go of old beliefs, distractions, and artistic blocks to find original solutions.
- Play, learn, and advance on your true soul path.
- Love your art-making process.
- Learn to give Intuitive Creativity Coaching Sessions.
- Formulate a Creative Action Plan.
- Coach yourself and others to an abundant life and success.

How This Book Is Organized

In *The Creative Pendulum*, a complete workshop in a book, you'll learn:

Chapter 1: How divining, healing, and creativity intersect and weave together.
Chapter 2: How to divine (or dowse) with a pendulum.
Chapter 3: How to divine with the Intuitive Creativity Charts (Table of Charts and Charts 1–2).
Chapter 4: How to use clearing and chakra balancing (Charts 3–4).

Chapters 4 through 12: How to use the remaining Intuitive Creativity Charts with information and suggested questions for each chart. The chapters include centering meditations, dowsing activities, and writing prompts.

Chapters 13–14: How to coach yourself and others, and give Intuitive Creativity Coaching Sessions.

Chapter 15: How to use the fourteen art prompts for beginner artists.

Chapter 16: How to host your own Divine Creativity Cluster.

Exercises

At the end of every chapter are Experiential Exercises.

- The dowsing exercises are sample questions to ask for each specific chart described in the chapter. You can reproduce this page for a quick reference as you learn to ask and receive answers from the Intuitive Creativity Charts.

- The journaling prompts give you time for inner reflection. Record them in a journal and also record other dowsing experiences. An inexpensive 8 1/2" × 11" spiral notebook will do.

- Chapter 15, "Paint on Your Hands: Art Prompts," has exercises for beginners to open to their inner artist and get messy.

Notes

- I devised the Intuitive Creativity Charts using specific words meant either to be factual or metaphorical, a way to light the creative path, and to help you discover your own desires and passions.

- I use the words *divining* and *dowsing* interchangeably throughout the book.

- I use the terms *Higher Power, God, Goddess, Spirit,* and *Great Creator* interchangeably to denote the Great Creator, the Source of

All, who in truth, is unnameable. There are many other names for God. Please feel comfortable replacing your own name for God as you read this book.

- I use the term *High Self* to denote that part of us that is divine and connected to Spirit.

- I asked for and received clients' permissions to write about their wonderful and profound stories. I have changed some names and a few details out of respect for client privacy.

- I also use experiences from my own life to further your understanding of the many processes used in this book.

Finding the Tannery Artist Lofts—My Spiritual Home

I have experienced many professional and transformational shifts in my life—from teacher to businesswomen to spiritual counselor to artist. Then I transitioned to living in an intentional artist's community in Santa Cruz, California.

In 2008, many months after losing my contract with *Memoir Literary Journal* and subsequently job hunting from Monterey to Marin in California, and with my house on the market, I was terrified of losing every material thing and being homeless.

When my car died, I bought a larger Suzuki Grand Vitara (what a name for my next adventure) just in case I had to live in it. Of course, I didn't tell my grown children, then in college, that I was so frightened. But living in my car was my backup plan. I wanted to escape to Santa Fe, New Mexico. I had heard artists were there. I wanted to be anywhere but where I was in the midst of that months' long crisis.

As all of this was happening, I didn't know where I was going or how it would all work out, but I trusted enough to keep following the many signs of Spirit, using my support group to stay sane, and in the morning, faithfully journaling, meditating, and exercising. I would then dowse with my Intuitive Charts, which always said "patience and courage," and I would talk with the angels in my meditation. In my journal they said, "All is well." Or when difficult days lay ahead, "All is swell," but it was rough seas for a long time.

My husband, James, had died ten years before. I had raised my children through their teens, ran my high-tech marketing company, downsized after the 2001–2002 recession, kept food on the table, and somehow paid the high mortgage. I laugh as I write—I don't know how I did it, except with help from sisters, other single moms, boyfriends, strong angels, and the grace of God/Goddess.

One day in April 2008, I saw a two-inch by three-inch ad in our local Santa Cruz *Good Times*—"Lofts for Artists." I said to myself, "I'm an artist." I had self-published two books, and now I was madly painting on canvas in my kitchen. I had also sold paintings in the Boulder Creek, Scotts Valley, and Capitola Art and Wine Festivals, to private parties, and had numerous café showings.

During those months of uncertainty, painting had saved me. I had found a new connection with Spirit. I had watched my girlfriend pick out Golden acrylic paints. I loved her paintings and was envious. She could say everything on a canvas in one painting that would take me a whole book to write.

When I had a dream that I was in too small a box and that my head was touching the top of the box, somehow I knew exactly what to do. I drove down the winding highway from Boulder Creek to Palace Arts (our local art store) in downtown Santa Cruz.

Shyly, I walked into Palace Arts and picked out a few colors using my intuition—magenta, yellow, white, and turquoise—a package of paintbrushes, and a few very small canvases. I drove home with my new materials and for nine months I painted. My paintings grew in size and complexity. I couldn't wait to wake up in the morning to see what Spirit was going to paint through me. Instead of focusing nonstop on my latest debacle of job hunting and imminent house loss as house values plummeted, I painted. Then I began selling my paintings for a little extra money at cafes and at art festivals.

When I saw the small ad for the Tannery Artist Lofts, I called the phone number and was directed to an office to pick up an application. Over the months, I kept calling and asking questions, until one day an exasperated clerk said, "If you really want to live here, you need to come twenty-four hours ahead of time to get a place in line for a loft in the Tannery." Ah, insider information! I was fifty-seven, a middle-class, college-educated woman with my own now-unaffordable home, but now I was going to be vying for low-income artist housing. I felt humbled and frightened, but girlfriends and sisters urged me to go for it!

Standing in Line at the Tannery Artist Lofts, Santa Cruz

In October 2008, I was in my new forest green rain suit that I had bought the night before. It was raining buckets, but I was a prepared Girl Scout. I was standing behind a woman who looked like I felt—soggy, covered by a hooded oversized jacket, and with a big black umbrella. Probably, like me, she was dreading the next twenty-six hours until we could hand in our housing applications. It was 6:30 a.m., a Santa Cruz Sunday morning. A group of us were across River Street from the not-quite-built-yet Tannery Lofts. We had come early, along with fifty or so others, and were waiting to form a line across the street in the parking lot.

I introduced myself, and peering out from the dripping umbrella, the woman, who looked my age, said, "I'm Rachel. Beautiful weather, isn't it?" I laughed and suddenly knew I was going to be okay. We were both holding folding chairs for the long sit-in along with duffle bags, sleeping bags, and tents.

I whispered, "I've never done this before. But I'm desperate."

"Me too. I need housing in Santa Cruz. I'm a dance instructor at Cabrillo College, and I can't afford to live anywhere."

I told her, "My house is in foreclosure in Boulder Creek. I lost my job. It's getting scary."

"What's your art form?" Rachel asked.

"Painting and writing now. I was a businesswoman! Oh my God! I was once employable and had a paycheck."

We looked around. There were more people now, a sea of different-colored umbrellas, chairs, and camping equipment. These people were just like us—needing housing. Then everyone in the line was talking, chitchatting, a wave of friendliness seemed to move up and down the line. The rain was letting up.

Suddenly, we were given the sign to cross the street. We did the hustle—grabbed our belongings, jostling each other, and made sure we had our place in line. A few minutes later, we were seated in a crooked snaking formation. An official carefully gave us a paper bracelet with our number. Rachel was number forty-nine, and I was number fifty-one. There were one hundred lofts. We felt more assured we'd be able to rent a loft. We snapped a photo with our phones, our wrists held high to commemorate our victory—already fast friends.

Almost Home

It was a bright and sunny Saturday morning in early February at the Tannery Artist Lofts. My shy and somewhat aloof nineteen-year-old daughter, Danielle, and I were standing in another line at the foot of the building stairs. I had been handed a half pencil and a half sheet of paper to write down our preference for a specific loft.

We had the privilege to choose our loft! We were elated.

All of us in line had been waiting for this momentous day—to actually see the just-built apartments and to be inside the Tannery Artist Lofts. We had been told in a letter and in person, "Even though you are here today and have passed the financial and artist interview, there are no guarantees that you will get a loft." But I reminded myself, we have made it this far.

Suddenly, we were allowed up the stairs and into the halls. I had a list of still-open two-bedroom lofts. Danielle and I started at the bottom and worked our way up, and on the third floor we found a stunning unit with eighteen-foot ceilings and stark white walls. It had a wall of windows that overlooked the San Lorenzo River and ceilings with unusual angles and exposed pipes. We took photos, including one of me, arms raised in my victory pose. Danielle said, "Mom, I'll take the front room with a door. I need privacy!" *Oh, she's getting interested, a little excited too*, I thought.

Over the days and from that Saturday onward, I prayed all the time. "Please, please, please and thank you for my new loft. Whatever you choose for me. It's fine!"

On a Monday, February 23rd, the angels would not leave me alone. "Pack, Joan. Pack more boxes." I was in a frenzy. I took a moment and looked up to say, "Okay, I'm packing. I got your message."

Tuesday, while having coffee with a girlfriend, I got the call. "Would you like to come in Friday? Sign lease papers for a two-bedroom loft on the third floor of the building?"

I replied, "Yes, but can I come tomorrow instead?"

The next day in the first-floor office, I sat down to sign the papers and handed over the deposit. At the last minute, they said, "Oh, we made a mistake." I took a breath and inwardly surrendered one more time. "We can reduce the rent by $200 a month. Would that work for you?"

Looking back, I'm still amazed I landed on my feet in an intentional artist community. How did this happen during a personal and nationwide recession and a financial meltdown?

How do I thank the angels, the Muses, the community of Santa Cruz County and an organization called Art Space, and the Tannery Arts, an organization that spent ten years planning and building affordable, beautiful lofts for artists? I keep on writing, painting, teaching and supporting the Tannery Arts' community. I keep dreaming of a world where everyone receives affordable, beautiful housing.

❖ ❖ ❖

In the first chapter we will begin our creative pendulum journey—one of discovery, freedom, and fulfillment—and yes, to the other side too, the lessons of frustration, anxiety, and resistance. But we can surmount all obstacles. Truly, you have been called. Let's learn to use the pendulum and then find your essential, creative self who embraces the magic, energy, and gifts. Together, we can transform.

A musician must make music, an artist must paint, a poet must write, if he is to be ultimately at peace with himself. What one can be, one must be.

—ABRAHAM MASLOW, American psychologist

CHAPTER 1

Where Divining, Healing, and Creativity Meet

Much of illness is a result of blocking the natural flow of an individual's creativity.

—BARBARA BRENNAN, American author and spiritual healer

At the Gathering of the Creatives Conference in Santa Fe, New Mexico, in 2018, a room full of open and eager people quickly learned to dowse with the Intuitive Charts in a one-hour class. After participants received instructions and began the exercises, the room was buzzing and alive. People were amazed at their own ability to move the pendulum and experienced their energy flowing through their hands and fingers. When they used the charts, they received inspiring, sometimes surprising, answers. Within a few minutes, they were helping each other by practicing and giving mini-readings to enhance their healing and their artistic lives.

If you who are new to divining (also called dowsing) with a pendulum, I want to reassure you that it's easy to learn. Dowsing is an ancient practice of using an instrument to ask questions and seek answers: diviners connect with their inner self and their High Self and Spirit to receive intuitive solutions. With the Intuitive Creativity

Charts, you can discover more than just *yes/no* answers (a binary system), and you can learn to research with the charts to receive multiple solutions and guidance for your creative life.

Divining with a pendulum, healing, and creativity intertwine and fuel each other. Over the last twenty years, I have been a psychic healer. What I have noticed is that as people heal from emotional and physical traumas, they naturally become more creative. It makes sense. As energy is healed and freed up from our past and present life issues, we have more vitality for our present lives. And as human beings, we as a species are both curious and creative, traits from our divine nature.

A powerful force exists within us that wants us to learn, grow, and expand. There is a High Self that holds our best aspirations and will take every challenge we may encounter to use it for good. We just need to be open to the Spirit within and without.

When dowsing, you naturally connect with your inner life and heal. While healing, you are led on a creative journey. As you discover, play, and learn, you begin your soul work. And as you practice divining with the pendulum and the charts, you become more intuitive; you will know in any given moment what is best for you and your creative life. This magical, circular process takes you into a deeper spiritual path.

As you heal, you are restored to your natural, innate self, which is imaginative and creative. Just watch children at play; they are developing motor, language, emotional, and social skills rapidly and in such original ways. Just as children have a deep urge to learn and express their creative selves, you too can feel that urge to transform and create. That desire is within you and is attempting to get your attention. Often that inner feeling of unease and discontent will pester you until you recognize it and take action.

You may suddenly want to change your life. You have an inner itch and are no longer satisfied with your life. You may not even know what you want to do or be when you grow up, whether you're twenty-five, just starting a career; forty, wanting a new career; sixty-five, just retiring; or seventy-five, or even older. You may discover inner desires lying dormant from childhood that emerge from your dreams, while journaling or while using the charts.

Gradually, you will hear your High Self and make changes to answer the call. These can be small changes—from buying a book to taking an art class to joining a writing seminar or an improvisation group. You could experience a larger transformation—going back to graduate school, moving to a new place, or starting a new career. Something powerful in you is moving, be it slowly or quickly, toward a new destiny. *The Creative Pendulum* will assist you in the search.

You will learn to dowse with the pendulum and with the Intuitive Creativity Charts, and that will help you discover your inner landscape and the artist within. I developed the charts to help you clear your energy, heal your soul, and guide you into the creative realm.

As you hold the pendulum and allow your energy to flow from your hand and fingers, you will find within yourself a place where the light pours in and you are connected to receive subconscious and superconscious answers from both your High Self and the spiritual world.

Over time, you will grow skilled in the use of the pendulum and charts, learning to give yourself and others readings and healings. Gradually, you will become more skilled and proficient.

I have included Intuitive Creativity Coaching forms and the one-page Intuitive Action Plan to help with your vision, intention, and focus to begin to enjoy the process and complete projects. You may also want to start your own inspirational group, utilizing all these amazing tools that transform lives.

After learning how to use the pendulum with the Intuitive Creativity Charts, you will learn the valuable skill of creativity coaching. To become a coach to self or others is a privilege, a sacred gift. As you encourage and see the growth in others, you will be able to see your own growth more clearly.

Come join us on this mystical yet practical path. You will find you are more authentic and alive than you have ever been, no matter what your age or circumstance. As you progress, you will find energy, excitement, and exuberance once again; you will find your innate, intuitive creative self.

Spirit Is Attempting to Get Our Attention

At some point in life, you may have grown restless and discontent. You may have encountered a deep desire for a more imaginative life. Maybe you have a wonderful family and a good job, but you know something is missing. Perhaps you tried shopping, buying a new car or house, and maybe even finding a new partner, but you still feel empty and lost. You may get help, perhaps counseling or coaching, but you have a need to go deeper. You want to feel free and passionate again!

Perhaps it was a more desperate time, as it was for my client, Dave, who was out surfing one day in Southern California after a job loss and divorce. A huge wave surprised him, tossed him up, down, and violently around, and he landed on top of his head. After a visit to the emergency room, it was confirmed that he was intact, though bruised, with a terrible headache. He just needed rest. He told me he felt grateful that he didn't have a brain injury or paralysis. I asked him what he thought the message was. He calmly said, "God is trying to get my attention!"

Like Dave, we sometimes find ourselves at the crossroads of life. You have been there, and I have too . . . many times. We may want to move forward, but we aren't sure in which direction to go and how we will find the means to change. Are you like Dave? Are you ready? Is God/Goddess attempting to get your attention?

What I Love About Divining with a Pendulum and the Intuitive Creativity Charts

- A pendulum is a simple tool—elegant and beautiful.
- It comes in many shapes and may be made of different materials and healing crystals.

- It is inexpensive, and you can even make one yourself.

- You don't have to plug it into a wall socket.

- Everyone can find a pendulum that they love.

- It neatly fits in the hand or pocket, and it can travel.

- You can quickly find answers . . . and sometimes surprising solutions.

- Through practice, you naturally become more intuitive, more creative.

- Divining with the pendulum helps connects you with your High Self and Higher Power.

- You can explore the mysterious inner world and open doors in the mind.

- You learn that you are not alone, that invisible forces are rooting for you.

- Using the pendulum with the Intuitive Creativity Charts, you are offered new ideas, extraordinary possibilities.

- Experiential Exercises.

Dowsing

If you do not already own a pendulum, go explore the world of pendulums! Multiple sites online offer them, or better yet, find them at your local crystal store or New Age bookstore. They are made in all shapes and sizes, and fashioned out of all different kinds of materials. The pendulum you are attracted to—the one that you find aesthetically pleasing—is the best one for you. See how it feels in your hand.

Later, after you have learned how to dowse, you can experiment with your pendulum, asking a few simple *yes/no* questions to see whether you receive a response. You will know whether the pendulum is a match for you. You can also use a pendulum to find a second pendulum, or if you are buying one for a friend, ask if it is a good match.

Journaling

- What made you pick up this book?
- What excites you about dowsing?
- What excites you about creativity?
- Why do you want to be more intuitive? Why do you want to be more creative?
- What do you imagine dowsing and a creative life could do for you?

Art

See Chapter 15, "Paint on Your Hands."

CHAPTER 2

Learn to Dowse with the Pendulum

I am an experiment on the part of nature,
a gamble with the unknown . . .

—HERMANN HESSE, German poet and author

People come to my pendulum workshops from all walks of life—men, women, young and old, in various professions—artists, therapists, teachers, healthcare workers, and high-tech professionals. They are curious about using a pendulum, a small weight suspended on a chain that can move to and fro, for dowsing and divining for their health, personal, creative, or business life. Just like you.

If you are craving a new creative lifestyle, or are a spiritual seeker, an artist, or all of the above, who wants a unique system to access your creativity and find guidance on your creative journey, you are in the right place.

When I arrived at my first dowsing class at my local Unity Church approximately twenty years ago, I had never heard of using a pendulum to heal or discover insights into my life. A friend had suggested I attend the workshop. She said there was an amazing teacher who was going to introduce us to a new mode of healing.

I had taken spiritual workshops over the years at the Unity Church. I loved them. I met like-minded people on their own individual evolutionary path. I always hoped the workshop would help further my relationship with Spirit and that I would gain connection, knowledge, and new tools. That day thirty or forty people met in the community room at our church.

Our minds were open to the experience, and we followed the simple instructions. We had a short meditation and, within a few minutes, all learned to dowse (divine) with a pendulum. It felt like a natural experience to hold and use the pendulum, almost as if I had used it in a previous life. I held the pendulum, and it moved all by itself. In the class we were all exclaiming: "It's moving. It works for me. How magical!"

Then we were given one chart to experiment with, and I practiced with it for an hour before bed that night. The pendulum still worked as I asked simple *yes/no* questions. I signed up for a more in-depth workshop the next day.

When you hold the pendulum, you first hold it still, making sure it can move freely. As you ask a question, the pendulum will begin to move on its own. The pendulum is responding to your nervous system through subtle body movements. When you are connected with Spirit, angels, and spirit guides, their energy can also influence the pendulum. When we ask a question about something outside of ourselves, we are sending out a request to universal consciousness. The pendulum acts as an antenna to receive information, and the mind becomes the receiving instrument.

Recently, I fashioned the Intuitive Creativity Charts (found in the Appendix) for use in my own psychic healing and coaching practice for clients and for guidance in my own life. Fun and easy to use, they inspire and motivate clients and myself.

In this book, I want to offer you that same experience of my first workshop. In this chapter, you'll find simple instructions to learn to dowse. Imagine I am with you, getting excited as I see your pendulum move. Know that Spirit is giving you the gift of dowsing and wants you to learn to use the pendulum.

How Does Pendulum Dowsing Work?

Honestly, we don't have all the answers to the question of how pendulum dowsing works. Though rod and pendulum dowsing has been scientifically studied for centuries in Europe and the United States, the question has not fully been answered.

Albert Einstein, when asked a similar question in a letter to a fellow scientist, said, "The dowsing rod is a simple instrument which shows the reaction of the human nervous system to certain factors which are unknown to us at this time." And yes, Albert Einstein, the world's foremost respected scientist, was a dowser himself.

What we do know is that dowsing has been used for centuries because *it works*. In China, the Middle East, Europe, and later the Americas, people have dowsed for water and minerals (called field dowsing), and more recently, for information (called information dowsing) on maps or charts. (See Christopher Bird's book, *The Divining Hand*, any edition, for a thorough history of dowsing.)

Dowsing has both scientific and mystical elements that help us tap into both our subconscious and super-conscious minds. Using the pendulum can help us to center emotionally and spiritually, and we can more easily open to a meditative state, where we become calm, relaxed, and receptive to the suggestions presented by the pendulum and charts. Time can be reduced between comprehending a problem and finding a wise solution to whatever dilemma presents itself.

Let yourself approach this new skill with an open mind, and let the curious creative self within play and let go. Some may learn quickly in a few minutes, whereas others may take more time. Later in this chapter, you will prepare for dowsing by doing a centering meditation, then I'll teach you how to use the pendulum, and finally you will learn how to use the pendulum with the charts. Yes, you too can, with patience and an open mind, learn to dowse.

When and Where Should You Dowse?

One of the best things about pendulum dowsing is that you can dowse anytime and anywhere. It's such a handy tool. But my own preferred time to dowse is in the morning after meditation. I find that if I've had a good night's sleep, I am naturally in tune with Spirit. If I don't have to rush off for an appointment, and I have time to truly relax and give myself the experience, then I feel my answers are clear.

Dowsing is an art form, and some days we might be more or less open to the presence of our High Self and Higher Power. If I'm grouchy or irritated from too little sleep, I may need to take more time to clear, center, and ground. Sometimes, just picking up the pendulum can be comforting when I'm disturbed. It's an outer sign that we are attempting to connect with our High Self and Spirit. The pendulum is a reminder of a spiritual connection that is always there and to which we can become receptive in a moment.

If you are emotionally upset, it's not a good time to dowse. Wait until you feel more yourself and centered, and then work with the pendulum.

Centering

Use your own meditation or the following "Centering Meditation" to relax and prepare for dowsing.

Take two to three minutes to center yourself before beginning to dowse. By centering, we bring our consciousness to our breath and the body, and we attempt to quiet the busy mind. As you take time to do this, your mind will naturally calm down and find its center. Afterward, you will be ready to use your pendulum, do research, and be prepared to receive correct answers.

It's a good idea to turn off your phone and set a timer. That way, you can truly let go.

Centering Meditation

Close your eyes and take a few deep breaths. You might want to let out a few sighs or noises ("ah, ah"), and let your shoulders relax. Then, either out loud or to yourself, ask your High Self, your spiritual guide, or Spirit, to be with you in your mind, heart, and soul.

As you continue to breathe, consciously lower your shoulders and ask your body to relax. Move your consciousness to your toes and wiggle them. Feel your feet on the ground. Breathe slowly and rhythmically, and feel your chest moving up and down as the air enters and leaves your lungs.

Inwardly, say a short, calming, affirmative phrase. For instance, "I am relaxed and at peace." Or "I am ready to have fun using my pendulum." Repeat the phrase, saying it slowly for two to three minutes until you feel centered.

When your mind meanders off into thoughts or worries, simply bring it back to the breath and affirmation. When your timer rings, give yourself a few seconds, wiggle your toes, stretch, and open your eyes.

Call In Your Spirit Guides

I always begin a dowsing session with a simple prayer, calling on my spiritual guides, calling on the angels of light and love, the archangels, and Jesus and Mary. The prayer can be very simple: "Please help and work through me." Then I notice I have lots of assistance! When I close my physical eyes and see through my third eye (the mystical center of intuition and wisdom located on the forehead between the physical eyes), I see my angels sitting on the sofa or above in my loft. Seeing the angels there is reassuring, and it's verification that my dowsing is providing my clients accurate and illuminating information.

If for any reason you become afraid, call on Archangel Michael and Jesus and Mary or your spirit guides for protection, reassurance, and refuge. Put down the pendulum and charts. Wait until you feel safe again.

How to Use the Pendulum

When you first learn to dowse and align with your subconscious and super-consciousness, it is surprising, even elating, to first view as the pendulum moves seemingly of its own accord.

Anyone can learn how to use a pendulum. It is a natural, God/ Goddess-given skill. It is important to suspend the belief that you can't. Instead, simply imagine that you can learn to do this easily. It's sometimes helpful to say a few affirmations, such as

- Spirit loves, guides, and protects me.
- Learning to use the pendulum is fun, easy, and safe.
- All subconscious resistance and blocks on all levels are now being removed.
- I am open and receptive to learning to divine.

Then follow these simple directions:

1. Center yourself and relax. (You can use the previous centering meditation.)
2. Check in with yourself and ask, "Am I ready to dowse?"
3. Hold the chain between your thumb and first finger. Make sure the chain hangs down four or five inches. (In the beginning a shorter chain is easier to use.)
4. Let the pendulum hang still.
5. Now we will train the pendulum to move and give you a *yes* answer. Keep your fingers, hand, or wrist still, and mentally ask the pendulum to move in a forward/backward movement or in the north/south direction. This movement is your *yes* answer. Then mentally tell the pendulum to stop moving.
6. Practice mentally saying the word *yes* and naturally moving your pendulum forward and backward, just as your head naturally moves up and down and nods *yes*. Do this a number of times until you are comfortable knowing that your pendulum is saying *yes*.
7. Mentally tell your pendulum to move side-to-side or in the east/west direction, just as your head will move back and forth when you mean *no*. This is your *no* answer.
8. Then tell your pendulum to stop moving.
9. Practice asking questions with *yes* or *no* answers. Start with simple questions that you know the answer to while you are training your consciousness and hand to dowse.

10. Continue to allow the pendulum to move without your hand influencing the decision. You may want to practice for a few days by asking *yes* or *no* questions before exploring the charts. If you feel you are ready, jump in and use the charts immediately. See how comfortable you feel and move at your own pace.

11. Expect a response and be in a receptive state for answers. Dowsing is a bit of a sister to faith.

(From *The Book of Pendulum Healing*, pages 23–24.)

If You Are Having Problems

Imagine I am with you in a workshop. I am clearing and helping you center, let go, and dowse. I am here with you now. You have a creative child within. Let go; let the child take charge, and visualize yourself easily learning the *yes* and *no* and clearing signals. Perhaps you have performance anxiety. Yes, we can all have it. Affirm the following sentences several times to clear your mind of skepticism:

• Dowsing is the Divine's gift to me.

• Dowsing is for my highest good and the good of others.

• I completely erase all doubting thoughts now.

• I easily and quickly learn to dowse.

Remember, this is an enjoyable process. If you get frustrated, relax and try again later. Try dowsing early in the morning or evening when you have plenty of time and space. After practicing, dowsing will begin to come naturally.

How Long Should You Dowse For?

You have to be a little careful, especially in the beginning, not to overdo the dowsing. No more than two hours, to allow yourself time to recharge. Dowsing brings in powerful, transformative energy, so be gentle with yourself.

Experiential Exercises

Dowsing

Practice with your pendulum every day, for a week, so that you become comfortable using your new intuitive tool. First, practice asking *yes/no* questions. For instance:

My name is _____.

I live in _____.

I am a _____.

Should I write today?

Should I paint today?

Should I dance?

Should I practice my music?

Is _____ the right color for my painting?

Is my painting finished?

Journaling

- Were you able to use the pendulum? Any blocks? Breakthroughs?
- How did you feel when you began using the pendulum?
- What surprised you?

Art

See Chapter 15, "Paint on Your Hands."

CHAPTER 3

Divine with the Intuitive Creativity Charts

(Charts 1–2)

What we play is life.

—LOUIS ARMSTRONG, American jazz trumpeter and vocalist

As you begin to explore and use the pendulum with the Intuitive Creativity Charts, you will be amazed how easily you will receive answers and guidance about a myriad of questions you might have about your creative life. In this and the following six chapters, I introduce the thirty-three charts with simple instructions and sample questions to ask, plus exercises to help you warm up. Take some time and turn to the Appendix to become familiar with the charts.

I developed the Intuitive Creativity Charts to help you research your own creative challenges and solutions. At first, they might be a little overwhelming for you. However, as you become more comfortable with using the pendulum with the charts, you will see that they flow in a natural order and allow you to research more quickly. The Table of Charts acts as a guide to the other thirty-three charts.

You are training your mind, body, and the pendulum to work with the charts. As you practice, the subconscious, conscious, and super-conscious aspects of your mind are working with Spirit, searching for clues and receiving answers.

Ask the Right Questions

Crafting your questions carefully is important. The pendulum can be very precise. If the questions are too vague, the pendulum might not move at all. If you're having problems receiving a clear answer, review your question and rewrite so it is as specific as possible. Writing down your questions can also be helpful so that you can see in black and white that your questions make sense, and if this is truly the question you want answered.

Clearing and Asking for Permission Before Beginning to Dowse

Before beginning, it helps to double-check that you are ready to dowse. Using your pendulum, ask:

- Am I working with my High Self and Spirit?
- Am I clear? (You will learn how to do this later in the chapter.)
- Are my answers accurate?
    - If the answer is *no*, center and clear until you are ready.
    - The answer should be *yes* before you continue.

When doing a reading for another person, always ask:

- Do I have the skill to dowse for this person?
- Is this for the highest good for this person?
- Do I have permission to dowse for this person?
    - If the answers are *no*, say a prayer for them and see them surrounded by God/Goddess, love, and light.

The British Dowsers sum up this concept by using the pendulum and asking:

- Can I? (Do I have the ability?)
- May I? (Do I have permission?)

- Should I? (Is it for the highest good of all?)
  - If you receive a *yes*, proceed.

Research: Finding Answers on the Intuitive Creativity Charts

After learning to dowse, turn your attention to the charts to help you ask and receive answers. Each chart is a little different, so I've included instructions with information about each chart, along with sample questions to ask.

1. Examine the Table of Charts, which leads to all the other charts. Place your pendulum over the middle of the black circle on the indicated chart. (My friend calls it the bull's-eye.) You can practice by asking a general question, such as "What do I need to know today?" Your pendulum will begin to move toward an answer. Then you can proceed to the next indicated chart.

2. Hang your pendulum over the black triangle or circle. Hold it there as you ask a question of the chart. The pendulum will start moving in the direction of the answer.

3. To double-check your answer, place your pendulum over the selected word. If the answer is correct, it will start spinning clockwise. You can literally feel the energy of the word.

4. Then return to the Table of Charts and ask a second question.

It is a good idea to methodically go through all the charts one by one. As you become familiar with them, your subconscious will remember them. Practice is key. As you learn and practice, you will begin to trust your answers and the pendulum.

Especially when you're new to dowsing, it's as if your pendulum has a mind of its own. So, just as if you were training a puppy, you must be firm. If your answers don't make sense:

- Ask to be shown only one answer at a time. Ask for the most important answer on the chart to be revealed.

- If the response seems totally off base, review these questions:
  - Is my question precise?
  - Am I working with Spirit and High Self?
  - Are my answers accurate?
    - *If the answer is no, keep clearing until you are ready.*
    - *Recheck your question to see if it is specific and the true question you want answered.*

- Sometimes the answers don't make sense in the moment, but in the future, they will! Write your answer in your journal, and see whether it makes sense later. This also happens in the spiritual readings I give. Sometimes the answers only make sense in the future.
- If you feel frustrated, take a break. Then come back to the process when you are relaxed and ready.

Yes/No and Clearing Chart (1)

For the beginning dowser, the Yes/No and Clearing Chart is the best place to start. You will become more comfortable with your pendulum and practice the *yes/no* signals and clearing signals.

We have many choices and make many decisions every day. According to Dr. Joel Hoomans, we make 35,000 decisions a day (*https://go.roberts.edu*). Now, that's a crazy number, but it illustrates that we do make a lot of decisions, some more important than others.

If you're a visual artist, you are constantly making decisions about line, form, color, and unity. If you're a writer, you're making word and editorial choices continually as you write. If you're a jazz musician, you're in a flow, making myriad choices in the moment to help your community of musicians sound great.

Chart 1 will help you learn to train your pendulum (remember, just like a puppy) to find *yes/no* answers. Just place your pendulum in the center of the circle, and as you learned in the preceding chapter, the *yes* signal is to and from your body in the north/south direction, just like nodding your head up and down, and *no* is side-to-side

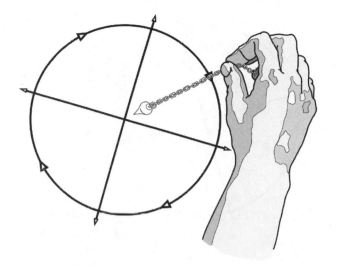

or in the east/west direction, like shaking your head side-to-side. (See the above illustration.)

After using the pendulum for a short while, you will no longer need this chart, but I still like to use it when I'm making an important decision to double-check and verify my signal.

Yes/No Answers

1. Center yourself.
2. Hold your pendulum between your thumb and first finger.
3. Hold your pendulum over the center of Chart 1.
4. Ask questions that illicit a *yes* or *no* response.

How to Clear

Pendulum clearing is a one- or two-minute process to lighten and enliven your thinking and cleanse your energy. In life and work we can sometimes pick up negative, confused thoughts that can muddle our minds and cloud our auras. These can be either our own or other people's thoughts, ideas, and expectations, or we can move too fast in life and become scattered.

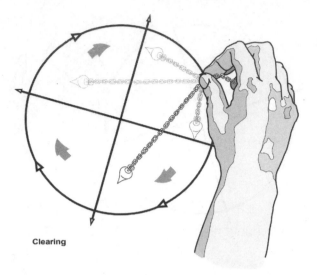

Clearing

Why clear? It feels good, like an energy shower. You may feel unmotivated to begin work or a creative project, but with a chakra clearing—pronto, presto—you're ready to begin. And when we use the pendulum and clear, we are tuning in and aligning with the universal life forces.

By using the pendulum, you can clear and refresh energy for yourself and others. You merely say, "In the name and through the power of Spirit, I ask for clearing for myself. Please clear me completely from all stuck, dark, or harmful energies no longer needed. Please fill me with light, love, and joy." If our energy in our own body is clear, then our intentions can manifest, and we can work efficiently and well.

Start with Chart 1 in the Appendix. To clear:

1. Ask your pendulum to move in a clockwise position.

2. Your pendulum will begin to move in a clockwise circular motion.

3. When your pendulum goes counterclockwise, take that as a sign you need a very thorough clearing. Let your pendulum move counterclockwise, and then it will start to go clockwise.

4. As it does so, ask the pendulum and Spirit to clear your mind, thoughts, and energy.

5. The pendulum will move and circle. (See the illustration on page 28.)

6. When your pendulum stops, you know you are cleared. You will feel a bit sharper and more awake.

Time and Percent (Chart 2)

Time

You may want to know when an event is going to take place because certain decisions could be made more easily if you knew. You can use the Time and Percent Chart (2) to find out the general timing of an event.

On the inner spokes of the chart, there are the words *day(s)*, *week(s)*, *month(s)*, and *year(s)*. On the inner curve, there are the words *past*, *present*, and *future*, and on the outer curve, there are numbers (10–100). You use all of them separately.

For instance, you might ask, "When is my contract going to come through?" The pendulum would answer by first by pointing to a day, week, or month.

Then dowse for the number, and it will answer with a number from ten to one hundred, which can also represent a single-digit number or a one, a multiple of ten. For instance, "10" can represent "1" or "100" and mean "1 month" or "100 months."

When you are asking about time, know that you are asking about the likelihood of something happening, based on events in the present projected into the future, which can always shift, because people do have free will, and they can change their minds.

Percent

Not only do we want to know when an event is going to take place, but we'd also like to know the likelihood of it taking place. With Chart 2 you can ask, "How likely is it that this will take place?" Or "How successful will this event be?" When looking for an answer asking for a percentage, you use the outer numbers on the curve 10–100.

Again, percentages can change, because people change and circumstances shift. Because we are constantly creating our own reality and others are creating theirs, predicting time and actions can be difficult. The universe is fluid, not fixed. Know that this is a general answer rather than a final one.

Experiential Exercises

Dowsing

Practice with your pendulum asking the following questions:

YES/NO AND CLEARING CHART (1)

- Do I need clearing? (If yes, practice clearing yourself.)
- Am I now clear?
- Am I ready to learn to dowse with the other charts?

Practice clearing with this chart, and practice without using it!

TIME AND PERCENT CHART (2)

- What is the general time frame of this event, project, or situation?
- How soon will I hear about ____?
- What is the possibility this event or situation will happen?
- How successful will it be?

Journaling

- Is using the pendulum with the charts easy or difficult for you? Why or why not?
- How does it feel to be clear? Can you tell the difference between being cleared and not?

Art

See Chapter 15, "Paint on Your Hands."

CHAPTER 4

Clear Your Life and Balance Your Aura and Chakras

(Charts 3–4)

When I first learned to dowse and gave myself spiritual coaching, I began naturally clearing everyone and everything in my life—children, animals, classes, house, car, office, stores, and myself. I became more sensitive to the energy around me, and I could feel blocked, negative, or weird energy. I learned to just clear it so that I could stay balanced for my life, my children, and in my work. What a powerful tool; what an amazing gift!

As I read more about healing, I realized I could clear my own and my clients' auras and chakras using the pendulum. Originally, I used my hands to clear, balance, and heal people's auras and chakras. But I like the pendulum because I can stay neutral, the client is more comfortable, and the pendulum can be used remotely for healing. The effect of clearing with a pendulum is the same or similar to clearing with the hands.

Most everyone is sensitive to others' energy to some degree. Sometimes you can walk into a room and know an angry person is there—perhaps a tired clerk or customer. You might leave immediately or intuitively because the energy doesn't feel good and can be detrimental to your well-being.

It's important to remember we can clear our outer environment and balance our own personal energy so that creativity can flow. Charts 3 and 4 help further pinpoint where clearing is needed and where in the aura and chakra clearing and balancing are needed.

Clearing Needed (Chart 3)

Clearing is a shortcut to healing, life, and art. I always tell my classes: if you were to learn nothing else except how to clear, you would have learned one of the most important aspects of using the pendulum. This chart clarifies what needs clearing in your life and, with the help of Spirit and your pendulum, you can clear people, places, and things.

- To clear others, remember to ask permission: "Do I have the skill to clear this person or environment?" "Is this for the highest good for this person?" "Do I have permission from the individual to work with them?" If you receive a *yes* answer, proceed. "In the name and through the power of my High Self and Spirit, I ask for clearing of ———."

- To clear a space or a place, whether your art studio, office, or house, you can draw a simple map from a bird's-eye perspective and hold your pendulum over the map. As you move your pendulum around the map, your pendulum might begin to spin. This is a sign that there is negative or stuck energy. You just need to ask Spirit and other guides to help you clear it. I use the simple prayer, "In the name and through the power of Spirit, I ask for clearing of this ———." Your pendulum will begin to spin, and it will stop when clearing is complete.

- In a similar fashion, you clear objects. If you buy used furniture, it's a great idea to clear them, especially beds, couches, and chairs, because they collect energy from the people who have used them before.

- I have also added clearing of "Aura and Chakras" to the chart, as well as "Self-Body," "Self-Emotions," "Self-Mind," and "Self-Spirit." Turn to the Aura and Chakras Chart (4) to pinpoint the issue and clear the aura and chakras. Then check and make sure you are clear on all levels—body, emotions, mind, and spirit.

- Perhaps you need to clear Negative Beliefs (found on Chart 7) or Distractions (on Chart 8).

You can also use candles (as old as time and used worldwide) to further clear a space and then bring in cleared crystals—such as citrine and rose quartz—to hold high energy. Again, if you haven't ever cleared, you might have a number of things on the chart that need clearing.

Imagine a cleared life where all parts of your life are working together for good and the energy is positive and open to your creativity.

Aura and Chakras (Chart 4)

While researching healing over the years, I became fascinated with the aura and chakras. The aura is the human energy system, and the chakras are the spinning wheels of energy that align with our spine. (Thousands of years ago the East Indians and Chinese identified these systems.) When the chakras are open and in balance, we feel happy, energized, and alive.

After I became a dowser and healer, and began giving readings to people, I first centered, grounded, and cleared my clients. Later, I realized I could also easily give my clients chakra clearings, which would greatly enhance their lives. Then, I began giving chakra clearings in all my spiritual readings, as well as my pendulum, writing, and creativity classes. These clearings seemed to release blocks and enhance learning and creativity.

If clearing the aura and chakras was good for healing, I knew it would also be great for creativity. I can feel the difference when I'm cleared and when I am blocked. Just this morning in meditation while dowsing, scanning, and checking on my chakras, I found my third chakra had a glob, a blob of darkness. I then cleared it with my pendulum. I wasn't sure where it came from or what it was, but I didn't necessarily need to know. Then—surprise—I painted for an hour before starting to work on this chapter.

When I give readings and clear a person's aura and chakras, I often see symbols, pictures, sometimes a person, and sometimes what looks like a little video clip in my mind. I report this to the client. If we have time and inclination, we can go deeper and find out more information. Present or past lives could be causing the blockage. We can then clear the aura and chakras so that the blockage doesn't hinder a person in this life.

When I cleared chakras for my client Margaret, we found that she was an African queen in one lifetime, and in another lifetime, she had even helped build megaliths in Africa. She had asked me for a clearing because she felt a little stuck in her artist life and wanted some inspiration. (She reported that she had always loved African dance.) Soon she was painting in a new rhythm and created an original series of deep blue and orange paintings inspired in part by the spiritual reading I had given her.

There are seven primary chakras and lesser chakras on the feet and hands. The chakras are funnel-shaped with the end point of the chakras aligning to an inner channel of light. They are about six inches in diameter and protrude about an inch in front and back from the body. The following chart lists the colors, traits, and the energy associated with the chakras.

For artists, the sacral (second) chakra (seat of creativity and sexuality), and the throat (fifth) chakra (seat of expressive creativity and connected with the hands) are very important. Just by clearing these two chakras, exploring and focusing in meditation on these two chakras (see "Grounding and Chakra Meditations" at the end of the chapter), you may find you can unblock and enhance your creativity. But, on the other hand, all the chakras are important, and it helps to have them all in balance!

Clearing the aura and chakras will immediately brighten you up. Just put your pendulum at the triangle and ask, "What chakras need clearing?" Then ask your High Self and guides to clear you. You will see your pendulum spinning in a clockwise manner, and when it stops, you are cleared. If you've never had a chakra clearing, you may need to clear all of them. In the following sections, I offer a chakra meditation.

You will greatly benefit from aura and chakra clearings even if you are just learning about them. For more in-depth information, see *Wheels of Light* by Rosalyn L. Bruere and *Anatomy of the Spirit* by Caroline Myss.

Name	Location	Color	Associations
1 Root	Base of Spine	Red	Physical Body, Safety/Security
2 Sacral	Below Belly Button	Orange	Sexuality, Creativity, Feelings
3 Solar Plexus	Stomach	Yellow	Power, Self-Expression, Will
4 Heart	Heart	Green	Love for Yourself, Others, and Your Creations
5 Throat	Throat	Blue	Communication, Expression, Creativity
6 Brow	Third Eye	Variety	Intuition, Inspiration, Problem Solving
7 Crown	Top of Head	Purple	Connection with High Self/Alignment with Spirit

Before meditating, use the Aura and Chakras Chart (4) to discover any blocks in your chakras and to get in touch with the energy and power of each of the chakras. To get in touch with your aura and chakras, try the following meditations.

Grounding and Chakra Meditations

As you follow the meditations here, focus on each chakra, front then back, and ask the angels of light and love to clear away any dark or negative imprints and then to brighten and bring energy to each chakra. You can do this meditation sitting with or without your pendulum. If I use my pendulum, I clear the chakra as I meditate with my eyes closed. You can focus on each energy center and see it fill with light, clear, and be restored. Or you can physically touch each chakra point on your body and breathe, as you move up the body, which is very relaxing. You can record this meditation in your own beautiful voice.

Grounding Meditation

1. To ground your energy, place your feet on the floor.
2. Imagine little roots growing to the center of the earth and connecting with the Earth Mother.
3. Then send a taproot from your first and second chakras to the center of the earth that connects with Earth Mother.
4. Thank her and ask that her divine, healing earth flow upward into your feet, legs, and into your pelvic region.
5. Feel it flow up to the core of your body, into your chest, heart, and lungs, down and up your arms, into your neck and head, touch every cell, organ, bone, and part of your physical being.
6. As you inhale deeply, draw up this energizing, green, and gold healing light into body, soul, and aura.

Chakra Meditation

Now, for this meditation, start at the base of the spine and work your way up the chakras:

1. The first chakra in the pelvic region is the bright, earth red energy. Visualize this color giving you an energy bath

of life force. The color expands in your pelvis, flowing down your legs, and then filling your pelvic region, the core of the body, back, shoulders, and down the arms. Then the earth red energy moves up again to your shoulders, filling your head, spilling over into your aura.

2. Imagine the second, or sacral, chakra, related to sexuality and creativity, located in your lower abdomen, clear and fill with bright orange light. As you breathe into the sacral chakra, it expands and fills you with a powerful, creative energy.

3. The third, or power, chakra in your solar plexus is related to self-esteem and will. See it filled with bright yellow. Feel yourself empowered and determined to start, act, and complete your projects.

4. The fourth, or heart, chakra is related to connection and love. See this center expanding and flowing with pale or deep green and sometimes pink colors. See it fill with love for others and your own creations.

5. The fifth, or throat, chakra, which is related to communication with others and the self, opens and expands with a beautiful blue. Writers, speakers, and performing artists have an enlarged deep blue chakra. See your chakra as blue—deepening, expanding, and enlivening your creativity.

6. The sixth chakra, the third eye, related to intuition and insight, is indigo or sometimes a personal color of your choosing. I see third eyes of my clients as blue, brown, obsidian, or crystal light. Dowsers, psychics, and other healing arts practitioners have expanded third eyes. Focus on your third eye between your eyebrows. Clear it and see it fill with brilliant light.

7. The seventh chakra, the crown, is located on top of the head and is most often a beautiful purple color. This is where you connect with your High Self and Higher Power. I have seen spiritual people who meditate daily with strong purple and gold chains of light extending upward. Clear

your own chakra and see it fill with purple light. Visualize your connection with your High Self and Spirit.

8. As you finish, see a light that is white and green with a little purple, six inches above your head. See it showering you with this light, clearing your aura from the top of your head, down to your toes, and out to the tips of your fingers. See yourself in a bubble of healing light, love, and creativity, extending out twelve inches—protected and empowered.

9. To finish, bring your attention to your feet. Wiggle your toes and take three deep breaths. Open your eyes and give thanks for your healing.

You will feel much brighter after your color and chakra bath in which the angels have cleared you. What a perfect way to start and also end a day. Don't forget to thank your angels!

As you go back and forth between the charts and familiarize yourself with them, you are becoming a dowser. After researching, clear all by saying, "In the name and through the power of Spirit, I ask for clearing on all levels." Then, refill the energy by asking that love, joy, peace, and creativity be within you, others, and your surroundings, and that your will and Spirit's will be aligned.

Experiential Exercises

Dowsing

CLEARING NEEDED CHART (3)

- Do I need clearing?
- Does my space need clearing? My studio? The venue?
- Does my art, equipment, or instrument need clearing?
- Does someone else need clearing? (Remember to ask: Do I have the skill? Is it for their highest good? Do I have permission?)
- What else needs clearing?

AURA AND CHAKRAS CHART (4)

- Does my aura need clearing?
- Do my chakras need clearing?
- Which specific chakra needs clearing?

Journaling

- Did you notice any changes after you cleared yourself and your surroundings?
- How does it feel to be able to clear and shift energy?
- How does it feel to have a clear aura and chakras? Can you feel it? Did you notice anything different as you moved through your day?

Art

See Chapter 15, "Paint on Your Hands."

CHAPTER 5

Create Time for Morning Quiet and Inspiration

(Charts 5–6)

Creativity takes courage.

—HENRI MATISSE, French painter

When you start a daily practice of Morning Quiet Time (Chart 5) and Inspiration (Chart 6), you will be rewarded with a deeper, more enlivened life. Your intuitive powers will increase, and you will feel centered and ready to start another blessed day. If you do little else in this book other than institute a morning quiet time for finding connection with higher forces and inspiration on a daily basis, your life will transform naturally. The Morning Quiet Time Chart gives you fourteen options to take you into your inner mind and heart, and the Inspiration Chart helps you look inward, then outward to what moves your soul, sets your heart on fire, and wakes you up.

Morning Quiet Time (Chart 5)

Morning might become your most precious time. The early hours can be quiet, serene, and sweet. A time just for you and your Higher Power, a time to journal, meditate, pray, or dowse. Why morning? Perhaps because the needs of our productive, overachieving self haven't yet switched on or woken up. At this time, when we have a few moments with our soul, we can check in and find out our true needs and desires.

If you're like me, during my thirties, forties, and fifties, life was intense, busy, and exciting. Of course, that little word *busy* doesn't really describe the day-in and day-out responsibilities of a working mom with her own business and a mortgage to pay in California! But yes, busy! Often, the days flew by, and it wasn't until late at night that I slowed down. My morning time became ever more important.

You might have to get up earlier, hide from your partner, children, and maybe feed your cat or dog, but give yourself the gift of solitude. After my daughter, Danielle, grew up, she said, "Oh, Mom. We were not allowed to disturb your morning quiet time." If I can gift myself with my own time, so can you.

But why *morning* quiet time?

Isn't it best to grab a cup of Joe and start in on breakfast, lunches, and perhaps tackle the dishes in the sink? Sweep? Vacuum? Don't the bills need to be paid? Shouldn't you take out the garbage before everyone gets up? Throw a load of wash in and fold the one in the dryer? You get the idea. Household responsibilities and chores can eat up your precious morning time and never end. Whether you work in the house or outside the home, your busy work life is also calling.

Quiet time in the morning is a peaceful way to transition from sleep to waking and an opportunity for remembering those dreams or ideas that bubbled up from the subconscious the night before. By midday, you will be in a full run. In the afternoon, you'll be finishing up work and picking up your kids. In the evening, you'll be making dinner, washing the dishes, and watching TV. You might be saying to yourself, "I was going to journal, meditate, and dowse today, but I forgot!"

I've always believed in variety, and that's why I've offered these suggestions on Chart 5. Using the pendulum, ask what you should focus on that morning. Perhaps it is journaling. Then you can ask again. Prayer? Meditation?

I am able, before all the chatter starts in my head, to hear a plan for the day. It's a wonderful time to listen to Spirit and what She might have in store for today. It's a great time to write your affirmations or a gratitude list to reprogram your brain.

When I practice morning quiet time, I am more centered throughout the day, and events just flow. I am nicer to my partner, smile more, and am more patient (a hard one for me) with others.

You may have encountered many of these ideas offered on this chart before. I will just say a few words about each suggestion. You can mix and match and keep your morning spiritual practice strong.

Affirmation A positive statement said in the present tense affirms a hoped-for outcome. "I am whole, well, and healed right now."

Angel Message In your journal, you can ask your guardian angel or the angels of light and love for a message. It's amazing, but if you just wait patiently, you will hear words of love and encouragement, and your hand will begin to write.

Daily Action Item List My mom was a great list maker. Sometimes it's helpful just to write down what you think you need to accomplish that day. Ask the angels to help you get your daily work done. You might not finish all the things on your list, but by writing them down and releasing them to Spirit, you can use the power of intention and manifestation to accomplish all that you can.

Draw in Your Journal Drawing is such a dynamic practice to help slow us down, appreciate, and see in a more focused way the details of a plant, flower, or tree.

Gratitude List By creating a practice of gratitude, we remember our blessings and bring a more positive attitude to life. We draw to us all those things we are praising. It's a way to see the positive in all situations so that we might deal with the ups and downs that life throws our way. Every experience is a gift.

Journal There are many methods for journaling. My favorite is Julia Cameron's "Morning Pages" from the book *The Artist's Way*, where the goal is to write three pages of stream of consciousness to clear the mind. It's a free space to learn all about yourself—what you are thinking and feeling, what you want and need. Here, you can release and let go of any subconscious blocks and resistance to your life and art. This process is a bit mysterious, but it works. You will feel better afterward, know what you are thinking, and be able to move forward into the day.

Meditate There are many different ways to meditate, many paths to enlightenment. It's rewarding to explore and see what works for you. My favorite is grounding, breathing, and mindfulness. Repeating a calming or soothing word slowly to yourself—for instance, *peace* or *hush* or *love*—can help still the mind. Meditation is listening for Spirit; prayer is speaking to Spirit.

Message from the Muse Does she exist? Yes. I am not sure of her name, but I have received direct messages. She's always urging me to work on my projects, whether it's a book or painting. Sometimes my Muse will not leave me alone until I do what she tells me to do. I sometimes have to explain that I need to take care of life details before I can focus. But she is insistent and doesn't take no for an answer. I have learned to listen and follow her directions.

Pendulum Dowsing

As I said earlier, quiet morning time is a great time to dowse because we are more connected with our subconscious and super-conscious selves, and less with the ego/mind. I love using the charts to enhance my morning time. I keep my pendulum and Intuitive Creativity Charts handy, so if questions arise, I can ask immediately and receive concrete guidance.

Pray for Friends As I journal, I remember friends who are going through difficulties. As these thoughts arise, I say simple prayers asking for their highest good, that they be healed and loved, and that the grace and love of Spirit be with them always.

Pray for Self It's important to remember we can pray for ourselves. We can ask that God/Goddess hear our request for what is needed! It's so comforting to know and feel the Universal Spirit who wants what is best for us and who can heal all things!

Read Spiritual Books I love being in touch with other inspiring teachers whose books take me to a higher level.

Record Your Dreams Dreams are where the subconscious mind comes out to play and we are at our most imaginative. I love recording dreams and musing about their meanings. If I didn't like something about a dream, I can change it in a meditation and see a positive outcome. If the dream is calling for a specific action, I make sure I follow its guidance.

Self-Coaching In Chapter 13, you will find a complete system for self-coaching.

Inspiration (Chart 6)

I find I cannot live or work without inspiration. I need to find it, whether the impetus comes from a book or painting, or from Mother Nature herself. It's so much easier to live and create when I'm enthused and excited. Look daily for what lights up your heart in Nature and in art.

Julia Cameron teaches her "Artist's Way" students to go on weekly "Artist Dates," a time for visiting new venues—coffeehouses, art galleries, or museums. Or out in Nature—in the backyard, to parks, or hiking trails. Or shopping in art stores for a new color of pen or paint.

When I found myself leaving the house a bit jangled, I asked Spirit to guide me. She did—to a quiet bench beside the Pacific Ocean where I wrote with green winter grass below my feet and a sky full of wispy white clouds. Before me were the blue ocean waters, curling waves pounding rocks, white foam, and a flock of black cormorants sitting in the surf. Further out on the water, black-wetsuit-wearing surfers were attempting to ride the waves. I breathed in the salty cool air, calmed down, and picked up my pen one more time.

When I came home, I looked up the meaning of the word *inspire*. The dictionary listed two primary meanings: (1) to fill someone with the urge or ability to do or feel something, especially to do something creative; and (2) to inhale, which made me laugh. Spirit took me to a beautiful place where I could breathe and write. May you find the magical and the mystical in Nature, art, books, film, and other people, where you feel the presence and inspiration of the Great Creator.

The Muse Visits

On July 4, 2006, I was at the San Francisco Airport drinking coffee with my best girlfriend, Kyra. She had suddenly decided to move to Hawaii, and I felt abandoned. I had also lost a profound relationship in June! I was distraught and asked her, "What am I going to do with my life?" Kyra, a psychic and painter, checked inside her clairvoyant mind and announced, "You're going to write poetry." In that moment I did not believe her, as I had never written poetry before and it made no sense.

I instead was planning on reigniting my passion and love for my marketing business. I had just leased a small office full of light in Santa Cruz with a deck and slight view of the ocean. I was within walking distance of Seabright Beach.

But I had these intense feelings of love in my energetic being and didn't know what to do with them. Due to life circumstances, we couldn't be together. It was complicated!

That day I drove from the San Francisco Airport to Half Moon Bay and down the rugged, windswept California coast to Santa Cruz. I arrived at my office and began to write. Soon I was on my knees in my new little office, pouring out my raw feelings on paper, and then poetry fragments began to emerge. At some point I realized I was listening intently within for the words and poems. Two hours later, I ran downstairs to the coffee shop, Java Junction, and bought a double latte. What had happened to the time? Days went by, and I was still writing poetry instead of reenergizing my marketing company. A good friend said, "You know, you won't make any money writing poetry."

I tutored myself with John Fox's *Poetic Medicine: The Healing Art of Poem-Making,* which did help me sort, feel, and think about what I experienced. Then I asked my singer-songwriter friend, Dan, to help me edit the poems. Oh, there was a lot of red on the paper. I had a dream he was massacring my poems. I told him he was too rough with my poems, to be gentle. By that time the poems were like little healing beings to me.

For nine months I was often in an altered space, feeling very much under the guidance of this loving poetry Muse. I just thought about my little poems while driving or dancing at Jazzercise. Although I was missing words here and there, I just waited until the perfect word appeared. Sometimes when having coffee with friends, I would ask them, or they would just blurt out the word I needed.

I revisited all the romantic places I had gone with my lover—Seabright Beach, the whale sculpture beside the little Natural History Museum, and the Union Café in downtown Santa Cruz. I took digital photos, which soon became cover photos of my upcoming poetry book, *Catching You, Catching Me, Catching Fire*, published in 2005.

So out of grief, when I felt I had lost the love of my life, I wrote poetry—poetry that healed me. Dan took a few poems and wrote songs to go with them. After the book was released, Dan and I performed a night of poetry and songs at the Java Junction Coffeehouse.

Looking back, I remember feeling so open and passionate. Later, I was embarrassed about what I had done—writing and publishing a book of poetry about my failed love affair. I said that out loud?

But when I moved into the Tannery Artist Lofts, I read some of my poems at a "Tannery Talk." I was told that I inspired others to be honest about love and passion in the later years. I even inspired my girlfriend's art class of young students from Monterey Peninsula College. She had a frank discussion with them the next day. Then my friend, Deanie, and her lover, Happi, read and loved my book. Deanie wrote her own book of poetry in the last year of her life.

So, write. Write as if your life depends on it. It might. If you're lucky, the loving Muse will visit you, heal your heart, and your soul too.

Experiential Exercises

Dowsing

MORNING QUIET TIME CHART (5)

- What would be helpful for my artist within to do this morning?
- What would Spirit want for me?
- What else do I need?

INSPIRATION CHART (6)

- What do I need right now?
- What will inspire me to start?
- What would be a great "Artist Date"?

Write your own questions. What does your intuition tell you?

Journaling

- How did it feel to have morning quiet time?
- Are you beginning to look forward to morning quiet time? Why or why not?
- Did your day seem different having had morning quiet time?
- Record any other changes you might have noticed.
- What inspires you on a daily basis? What do you long for weekly?

Art

See Chapter 15, "Paint on Your Hands."

CHAPTER 6

What's Standing in Your Way? Uncover Negative Beliefs, Distractions, and Blocks, and Find Solutions

(Charts 7–10)

*To inquire about what prevents our creativity, it turns out,
is to reveal the essence of who we are and who we are
becoming or failing to become.*

—MATTHEW FOX, *Creativity: Where the Divine and Human Meet*

In this chapter, I introduce four powerful charts to help you examine your own negative beliefs, distractions, and blocks, and discover tried-and-true solutions to these pesky, persistent issues that are unconscious, deeply imbedded, and can seem insurmountable.

One of the best aspects about writing a book is that I am able to reflect and viscerally experience what I'm writing about. I must admit I was a little fearful of this chapter. I was afraid of negative beliefs, distractions, and blocks because at times they feel so powerful. But I am offering the tools to examine your mind together with reliable solutions that have worked for me. It's an ongoing process that will clear the rubble of your mind and enhance your own creative journey.

Regarding our negative beliefs—on any given day, we think thousands of thoughts. "In 2005, the National Science Foundation published an article summarizing research on human thoughts per day. It was found that the average person has about 12,000 to 60,000 thoughts per day. Of those thousands of thoughts, 80 percent were negative, and 95 percent were exactly the same repetitive thoughts as the day before" (statistics from the TLEX Institute report "Mind Matters: How to Effortlessly Have More Positive Thoughts," *tlexinstitute.com*).

If you are like me and seek out alternative approaches to traditional Western culture, with an interest in spirituality, mysticism, holism, and environmentalism, you know that negative thoughts and reflections of who you are (from infancy to present, and perhaps from past lives) can deeply affect your idea of what you can accomplish, and thus your behavior too. Some of us are in a small box with negativity bouncing off the walls at us. Now it's time to identify these negative beliefs so they don't control us, and then, from this higher perspective, we can choose who we truly want to be.

We must also consider the big, bad brothers—distractions and blocks—which will rob us of our creativity. What is the difference between a distraction and a block? They are probably on the spectrum together. Distractions prevent us from giving our full attention to someone, something else, or our creative work. In contrast, creative blocks can be mountainous and bar our access to our inspiration.

I really didn't understand creative blocks until I had been a writer and painter for years. I didn't acknowledge that creative blocks were real or valid. *Oh, that's an excuse*, I thought. *Oh, I'm being dramatic*. When I started writing my first book, I was overloaded with responsibilities, so it seemed natural that my writing would come in fits and starts.

With more time and experience over the years, I realized keeping inspired, active, and on track is almost a part-time job. You must keep removing negative beliefs, distractions, and blocks so that when you show up to the page or the canvas, the creative energy can flow easily through you. As the years go on and you're published, you've sold your artwork, and you're working full-time in what you love, you must still be aware of these inner monsters.

I wrote this chapter in 2020, during the first year of the COVID-19 pandemic. Even though we were sheltering in place, there was much to distract me, even while I was at home. I was attempting to stay put in my loft and work both at home and at an office a block away. My Jazzercise class was virtual because my gym was not safe, and most coffeehouses (where I also would write) only had outdoor seating. During this time, I had given up coffee and felt I couldn't think at all. Ironically, it's taken awhile to sit down and write this chapter—so many negative beliefs, distractions, blocks, and so little time!

The last chart in this chapter is the Solutions Chart (10), which contains many ideas and suggestions for blasting away the molehill or the mountain. I am sure, if you've been in the game for a while, you may have tried many of these—repeating affirmations, meditating, creating structure, and using several other techniques. Sometimes you might just need a little boost, and others times you may need therapy. My wish is that by using these charts, you will discover your own negative beliefs, distractions, and blocks, and uncover the many solutions that can work for you.

Negative Beliefs Chart (7)

One of the best exercises you can do for yourself is to uncover your core negative beliefs found on Chart 7. Once they are in the light, they will cease having as much power over you. To counter the effects of negative beliefs, you must clear them with your pendulum and insert positive affirmations into your consciousness. This should be a lifelong practice that becomes automatic. If you catch a negative belief in the moment, such as "I'm so silly. I can't possibly do that. What would people think?" you can say, "Cancel, cancel that thought." Then affirm, "I am a wise person. I can learn and try new things. I don't have to be perfect!"

I have wrestled with the following negative beliefs much of my life. Despite my mind at times blathering on, I have managed to create much in my life. I am still working on clearing negative beliefs, however.

- People will think I am bragging.
- They will know I am a fraud. I'm not a good writer, artist, or spiritual psychic counselor.
- My sisters will be jealous and hate me.
- If I tell the truth, I will feel ashamed.
- My family already went through difficult times. I don't want to hurt their feelings.
- My younger sister is the brilliant one, not me!
- I will go crazy, like my mother.
- I have no original ideas. All of them have been given away to other people!
- No one wants to hear what I have to say.
- I will be alone while I write, paint, and work.
- Under all this shame is a deep, dark well I won't be able to crawl out of ever.
- If I say it out loud, people will ridicule me behind my back.
- If I'm honest, I'll feel too angry. I will be banished.
- I will never have any real money because I don't deserve it.
- I will get ill. I will die if I finish my work.
- My lover will leave me if I tell the truth.
- I don't deserve success. That is for other people, not little me.
- It's too late! I am too old. My brain cells are dying.
- Blah, blah, blah!

After using the Negative Beliefs Chart (7) and discovering the lies you tell yourself, be sure to clear yourself with the pendulum.

You can also talk back to your mean thoughts in your journal. Defend yourself and tell them why they are untrue. Give them the hard evidence—what you have become and accomplished. How dare those meanies talk to you like that! Would you ever talk to a friend this way?

Here's what I wrote to and about my negative thoughts:

- People love hearing about my life and fun projects. I inspire, encourage, and motivate others in their creative lives.

- My sisters love me. They might be a little envious, but they soon get over it. The feeling of envy makes us aware of what we too would like to do or be or have. I support and inspire my sisters.

- When I tell the truth, I am stepping into my own power. Truth is my sanity and friend.

- My intention is not to hurt my family's feelings. I need and want to speak, express, and tell the truth. Only then will I know who I am and what my life experiences are.

- Yes, my younger sister is brilliant. But I have a different, unique brilliance inside of me. We all have our own gifts, talents, and journeys.

- Yes, my mother was bipolar and an alcoholic. But she didn't have the help she needed earlier in life to overcome her problems. At the end of her life, she found a sober and spiritual path, and helped start a women's recovery center in San Luis Obispo County that is still thriving today. I learned so much from my beautiful, creative, loving, wonderful mother.

- I combine the best ideas with my own way of teaching, coaching, and "arting." I am so very creative in my life, my work, and my art!

It feels great to communicate from your High Self to your earthly self. After this journal writing exercise, clear yourself of the negative beliefs with the pendulum. Ask the angels to clear you in every cell of your body, in your chakras and aura, and on all levels. Rip up the paper where you wrote down your core negative beliefs. Some people even burn them. I also send clients to the river, lake, or ocean to throw small pebbles into the water, those stones representing the false beliefs. This exercise helps release the feelings inside you.

Then, make a few copies of your affirmations and honor yourself by posting them and reading them aloud often. You can also write them ten times or more in your journal to embed them in your subconscious. Use the affirmations you have written in the upcoming collage exercises.

Ongoing: Stay conscious and keep clearing yourself with your pendulum when needed. Watch for changes in your feelings and beliefs. Thank your higher angels for all their help.

If caught in a dark mindset, call someone who believes in you. Tell on yourself: *This is what my crazy head was saying.* Be truthful with your friend. Then clear the thoughts. Hey, they're only thoughts, not the truth. Do a reset and reframe with your buddy. *Oh, I did write four books. Oh, I was in ten art shows. Oh, I did perform in front of all those people, and they loved me. Oh, I did show up even though I was scared to death. I am a writer and an artist!*

The Negative Beliefs Chart (7) contains a list of words that may be part of your negative mindset:

Abandoned	**DumbFat**	**Silly**
Alone	**No Ideas**	**Stupid**
Angry	**Not Brilliant**	**Too Honest**
Ashamed	**Not Enough**	**Too Late**
Crazy	**Not Smart**	**Too Old**
Die	**Other**	**Ugly**
Don't	**Rejected**	
Deserve	**Ridiculed**	

Let's banish them from our vocabulary and thoughts.

Negative Beliefs, Distractions, and Creative Blocks

I asked the following of fellow artists in my circle: "How do you manage your negative beliefs, distractions, and creative blocks?"

I try to work through them, rather than avoiding them. I let go of the fear.

—CATHERINE SEGURSON, founder of the *Catamaran Literary Reader*

With great difficulty. I meditate for five to ten minutes. I go for a short walk. I breathe. Walk around the living room several times. I have a tendency to go numb and get overwhelmed easily. (I will try techniques from your book!)

—PAMELA PAPAS, poet and stand-up comedian

Just keep working. Draw anything. Clean and organize the studio. Be disciplined about art as it is important work.

—MARGARET NIVEN, visual artist and college teacher

This is a great opportunity to ask oneself, "What am I upset about?" The negativity is usually birthed from a place of no art in my life. Or if there is something in the world that is bothering me, I ask myself, "What is it I want to say?" and then, "What would that look like for me?"

—MAHA TAITANO, sculptor and installation artist

I talk with other artists, and give myself better self-care.

—SANDRA SHAMMA, singer and songwriter

If I have really powerful negative thoughts about what I'm doing, I just give it a rest and work on another creative project.

—MARIA CHOMENTOWSKI, visual artist

I've been reading John O'Donnelly's book, *Beauty*. He says that having an encounter with the beautiful can move you from fear to courage. That thought reached me, so I'm trying to be receptive to beauty, in nature, in people, and in moments.

—HAPPI CAMPBELL, sculptor and painter

I'll go do other things for a while and clear my head. I'll trust that this is part of the process and that I'll eventually find my footing again. Once I'm on track, I'm generally obsessed and rarely distracted.

—ELIZABETH MCKENZIE, novelist

I find that if I don't write for a while, I start to feel out of sorts and unhappy. Writing poetry is as essential as breath.

—MAGDALENA MONTAGNE, poet and poetry teacher

Shut up, negative voices!

—DANI TORVIK, artist

Distractions Chart (8)

Distractions can be a minor irritation (like a siren outside) or more serious (like playing hours of video games). Just this morning, I had to force myself not to vacuum and scrub the floor. I don't even like housework, but I do like a clean house. I did sweep, do the dishes, and clean a table before I sat down to write. I wanted to do more, even though I knew the housework was acting as "resistance" to my writing. What is under that resistance, I asked myself. Fear. Oh, my old friend, I told myself I could do housework later, and I did.

You have to give the artist within permission to outfox that other self that tricks you and tells you, "No, no, whatever you do, don't start on your creative play and work."

What I learned is if you put your creative work first, then creative juices will flow and you will have easier days. All those duties and responsibilities will be there when you finish, and you will have accomplished the most vital task for the day.

Here is a list of common distractions found on Chart (8).

Alcohol Just notice if it's interfering with your work.

Cleaning Are you sure you need to clean out the closet now?

Crisis Maybe you are a crisis junkie. You like your own and others, and it keeps you in a state of excitement and anxiety. Perhaps once a crisis helped you fuel your life but, in the end, prevented you from doing your work.

Drama You love the drama! We all do. But it can suck you dry.

Drugs Like alcohol, drugs seem like magic initially, but later, they can turn on you.

Family Who do you put first? Can their issues wait? Can someone else help?

Friends Call them later, after work/writing/art-making time.

Housework Though I have never heard of a person dying because of cleaning, it can certainly be a distraction.

Internet Yes, I find the news, my favorite websites, fascinating. But check it later. Get to work. (Some authors work on a computer without Internet access, so they won't be tempted.)

Movies Limit your viewing if you can.

Noise Look for quiet spaces to work.

Organizing Yes, organizing is good and helpful. Some of us can't think without a clean desk. But if you find yourself arranging the towels in the cupboard by color and you're not doing your work, let it go.

People Don't let yourself get pulled into others' drama so that you don't complete your own projects.

Responsibilities Look at your responsibilities and see what you can do to minimize them so you have more time. Learn to say the short but powerful word *no* if anyone wants to heap more upon your shoulders.

Shopping Do you really need to go to the store right at this time?

Television The boob tube. Why? Yes, it's relaxing, but it is generally inane.

Unhealthy People This is a test. Are you spending too much time dealing with crazy makers who pull you into their dramas and prevent you from working? Consider minimizing your time with them and only in off-hours.

Video Games I am of a different generation and have never liked them. I feel they just rob children and adolescents of their time, and now, adults too.

Yard Work Great, after you complete your work, but not before.

But what about the bigger distractions that eat up all the hours of your time? Hours of Internet surfing, online game playing, and Netflix? The following short process can help you begin recognizing distractions and reducing their hold on you. Identify your top three distractions by using the pendulum with Chart 8.

1. Be honest with yourself and know we all face this battle.
2. Ask: "What is my primary distraction? What are two more distractions?"
3. Rate the distractions—from one being the least, ten being the highest—on how much they are preventing you from doing your creative work.

4. Track how much time you are spending on these distractions. Wouldn't you rather use this time for creative work and play?

5. Allow yourself to first do your work. Work first; then allow yourself some free time to play.

6. Set a timer. Then, jump back into your work when the timer goes off.

7. Reward yourself and give yourself gifts! Yes, it's a bribe! A new book, an article of clothing, a computer if you get that contract!

8. Stay aware. Your time is yours and precious.

Creative Blocks Chart (9)

Sometimes we don't even know we are blocked. We call our blocks other things—being lazy or undisciplined. As Julia Cameron says, "Blocked writers are not lazy." We may berate ourselves, hoping that will get us moving. Maybe we can force ourselves to work, but then our victory is short-lived, and again we are discouraged. Later we pick up the old habit and call ourselves worse names.

To permanently address our creative blocks, it is much better to root them out. They are tricky devils that must be uncovered, named, faced, and dissolved. Sometimes we have no conscious awareness. But when you name them while using the Creative Blocks Chart (9), you may suddenly have an "aha" moment! *I'm not lazy. I'm afraid. I'm afraid of ridicule.*

Here are the primary Creative Blocks found on Chart (9).

Addictions We use addictions to create blocks to our creative self. So many creatives in the past have fired up their work with alcohol and drugs. Writers such as Ernest Hemingway, Tennessee Williams, and F. Scott Fitzgerald, and painters such as Vincent van Gogh, Jackson Pollock, and Henri de Toulouse-Lautrec are examples of a few who suffered from alcoholism and drug addiction. Such a waste. It is a proven fact that you can be creative without alcohol or drugs and live a much better life.

Anxiety Worry or nervousness can be telling us we need to focus on our work. At first, I was feeling anxious and blocked because I was unable to get started on this book project, but then I started feeling this energy build for this work of art. This told me to get started immediately. Now I am writing. Anxiety is a message—so take action and begin. Paradoxically, anxiety can be both a solution and a block.

Busy Mind Breathe and focus and let every thing else go, except what you are working on in the present moment.

Childhood Trauma Our inner child may have been hurt by unconscious parents or teachers or other children. Sometimes we need a therapist to help us work through issues.

Criticism Who has not been stopped by indirect or overt criticism? A teacher in sixth grade, a guidance counselor in seventh grade, a college professor so mighty with a red pen, or an art teacher bent on attacking at least one student during a critique while praising other students. In academic settings and in the art and literary world, professional critics reign. Consider criticism a sign of being taken seriously. If you are decimated by the *New York Times* "Sunday Book Review," at least you were in the newspaper. Appreciate the instant critique on Amazon by your readers, and learn to use the feedback for improving your work. Always keep in mind that it is so much easier to criticize than to do the actual work of art.

There is a way in which to handle criticism and unblock. When being evaluated in person, always have a pen and paper handy and take notes about what is being said. Breathe and smile to raise your endorphins. Listen with your heart. By doing this, you are engaged in an activity; breathing and writing can capture the positive and negative comments. Too, you can always record it on your phone. Then later, you can evaluate with neutrality.

Know also who is evaluating you. You don't have to take criticism from everyone. Once, I was being let go from a job for a very strange reason, and on my last day, the boss offered to "critique" me. I said, "No, thank you."

Emotional Problems Yes, we all have emotions, because we are human and they make us human. But if our emotions are running amok, it's difficult to get anything done. Find what works for you so that you can process and learn from your emotions. You may need therapy, but you are not alone. When you finally get help and get down to work, you will notice you feel almost instantly better. When my clients are experiencing mental issues, I often refer them to a therapist. Many a creative, exploring the edges of their consciousness and pushing themselves too hard, have had to ask for professional help. It's almost a sign you are creative!

Fear Here are a few of the primary fears that you may face:

- *Fear of Failure:* Failure is such a loaded word and very heavy too. But failure can be celebrated, because if you fail today, learn from your mistakes, and don't give up, you will eventually succeed. Your success will be a victory and much sweeter. When I ran my high-tech marketing business, I made mistakes, large and small. After a hard day, I wished I could fire myself. Sometimes, I just wished I could quit, but I had children to support, not to mention employees counting on me. In the evening, I would tell myself, "I'm done." In the morning, I'd jog, journal, meditate, and pray; I'd ask for solutions and show up one more time.

  During the recession of 2001–2002, after a series of devastating events, including 9/11 and the dot-com crash, we lost hundreds of clients and 80 percent of our potential revenue in a short period of time. I was in San Francisco to meet a large income-producing client who canceled at the last moment. Instead of the meeting on that gorgeous day, I walked to a nearby church, got on my knees, and prayed. We reorganized, worked from our homes, and carried on. But that's also when I finished my first two books! When tragedy strikes, who knows what Spirit has in store for us?

- *Fear of Death:* When I was completing my last book, *The Book of Pendulum Healing*, I realized at the end of the process that I was afraid of dying if I finished the book. After all, this was a lifelong dream—to be published by a traditional publisher. I had worked on the book on and off and in some capacity for twenty years. If I finished, perhaps I had completed my goals and it was time to go to the other side. I, of course, didn't want to die; I wanted to live. So close to the end, I wrote in my journal and found out I had this block. I asked the angels and Guides to remove the block, and then I cleared myself.

- *Fear of Solitude:* I am a very social person. If I am alone, I some-times feel I don't "switch on." My inclination is to get out into the world and mingle. Before COVID-19, I'd go to my Jazzercise class, and after exercising, I'd have a conversation or two and then head home to work. When I lived in Venezuela, where I taught for a year, on Sundays I might have a whole day with no social interactions and plans to meet up with anyone. I remem-ber the feeling of intense loneliness, as if I were going to be swal-lowed by the quiet. But I had an art studio in my apartment, and I would just make myself go there. I would be lying if I told you it was easy to go there, knowing it would just be the Muse and me. Yet, even if all I could do was lay gesso on canvas with a big paintbrush, something would happen. I very much felt con-nected to Spirit and the Muse and no longer felt alone.

  You might have heard how dangerous Venezuela is—still today as I write. I was there in 2010–2011, and at the time, the kidnapping and murder rate was higher than Iraq's. Even though I attempted to be safe, I didn't really feel safe until I left that country. I was on the seventh floor of a high rise, but my front door had a metal gate in front of it. I had a small, older car, but my car often would break down. I'd run to the taxi stand nearby, but there were no taxis, it being rush hour, so I'd walk to the school a mile away by myself. It was crazy.

  Painting and my Muse saved me. I'd paint on the floor—it's just what I do—and suddenly I'd notice I was in the creative realm. I was encircled with a happy, easy, light force. My paint-ing became my refuge, and the Muse always came . . . as she is coming now while I write alone in this office. Today, I love the quiet, the emptiness. Soon, I know I will be there in that place where time and space almost disappear.

- *Fear of Success:* This slippery fear seems to come and go and can prevent us from reaching our full potential. It can whisper in your ear, "Don't send out that poem. Don't apply for that art show. Don't go to the studio. Don't check out the new art gallery in town. Don't attempt online marketing. Don't do social media. Don't show up. Be late. No one cares. Shouldn't you reward your-self with a day off instead of sitting inside writing on a gorgeous day? Shouldn't you stay up late with friends? Shouldn't you stop right now and quit this foolishness?"

Sometimes fear is pointing us in the right direction. I now understand that if I'm fearful of something, there is a powerful energy behind the fear. I have trained myself to say *yes* to what I am afraid of, because I know behind that fear is energy. After moving through the fear into action, I am always amazed that I was able to accomplish my goal.

A book I keep on my bookshelf is *The War of Art* by Steven Pressfield. He asks, "Are you paralyzed with fear? That's a good sign. Fear is good. Like self-doubt, fear is an indicator. Fear tells us what we have to do. Remember one rule of thumb: The more afraid we are of a work or calling, the surer we can be that we have to do it." Face your fears, and you will find new energy and abundance for your creative life.

When I was in the process of doing my first Facebook Live event, my wonderful musician friend John Michael said, "Another way to embarrass yourself." I laughed then, grateful for his ability to make me laugh and lighten up!

Inertia Are you smoking too much of that funny stuff? Just kidding. Sometimes the hardest thing is just to begin. One exercise from Eric Maisel's *Fearless Creating* is to put a drop of paint on a blank piece of paper. This exercise made me laugh, because in the process of just picking out the color of paint and the paper to put it on, you have begun. Then when you put down the paint, it's almost impossible not to paint.

SARK (Susan Ariel Rainbow Kennedy), inspiration author, coaches you to write down eight "MicroMovements" in a circular diagram. I love this brainstorming method because it also helps me break down my tasks, get moving, and at the same time, find the fun. The pandemic showed us that it's easy to get stuck on the couch (or bed)—how soft, how comfortable, how lovely. Do not let the allure pull you in and rock you to sleep. But sometimes that is maybe what you need. Dowse whether you should rest or work for a *yes* or *no* answer.

Inner Critic Related to the outer critic is the inner critic, who is alive and well in most of us creatives. Before I started doing spiritual work, I had an overpowering inner critic, a voice that disparaged me continually. Through counseling and recovery in twelve-step groups, I learned my inner critic attempted to keep me down with a running dialogue of what a terrible person I was. It was as if the inner critic built a box around my inner and outer life—"Don't go there, don't try anything new, stay home, ruminate, don't try that, and don't go to that event." Now, I tell her, "Thank you for sharing," and continue walking out the door.

That inner critic is still there, muted and quieter now. She actually helps me with my work. I gave her a job! I've turned her into the editor of my books—a more friendly editor and critic, who gives me good advice. But I don't let her judge my first drafts or my first attempts at any creative work. And she helps me see what I need to see in my paintings. I remind her, "Love and tolerance is our code." Yes, borrowed from Alcoholics Anonymous, but that is my code too!

Here is another trick. If you do something for the first time, you are off the hook. Your inner critic can take a break in attempting to improve you. The first time you try a new painting technique; take a class in an area you've never tried before; create an online class; write a poem; or do all the dowsing, art, and writing exercises in this book, you're off the hook. You don't have to impress or judge yourself or anyone else. You don't have to show or share with anyone if you don't want to.

Anytime you are learning anything new, you're off the hook. That means for an entire class or a whole year. How about you are permanently off the hook and everyone else is too? We are just here to explore, play, learn, and throw light into the world.

Inner Resistance At times this resistance can be subtle, little inner thoughts or, inadvertently, in a few words, someone discourages you. It might be much stronger and feel like a wall standing between you and your goal. When you declare to yourself and to the gods that you want to move forward with a project or you're right at the finish line, it's as if the Furies descend on you. Lost puzzle pieces, lost documents, or lost sound from a movie can delay our journey. Or computer software glitches and computer crashes can be enormous blocks and struggles. I just saved my document again.

You may think that because obstacles and events are obstructing the flow, it is a sign you should turn back. Instead, you can take this resistance as a positive sign—especially when it's the beginning or end of a process. It's more important than ever that you persevere. When you feel that force field pushing back, know you will have a breakthrough if you persist. Take it as a positive sign and keep moving forward.

Circumstances Force Us to the Next Level

I really enjoy teaching classes in person. They're small, intimate, and all of us get so close and learn so much from each other. But guess what? We experienced a pandemic, and I was forced by circumstance to teach online. The week before we were sheltered in place by Santa Cruz County, I had been investigating teaching online. Now I am fairly comfortable with it. Then I was asked to do a workshop online, a video talk, and then Facebook Live. As a result, I am reaching more clients. But fearful, yes! And yes, I had to ask for help. But God/Goddess and the angels of light and love sent me human helpers. Can you imagine—one was next door and the other directly across the hall?

Lack of Money Yes, I've been there, owing more than I had, and not knowing where the next mortgage payment was coming from. I've lost jobs, contracts, and money. But when I'm in that situation, where I don't know what's happening next financially, I begin giving things away from my closet and donating money, even a few dollars. I'm telling myself and the universe, *I'm so rich, I can be generous*. I've paid for medical appointments with paintings. If you keep heading in the right direction, resources appear, unexpected money comes in the mail, or you may win a scholarship.

Lack of Structure Especially when we have lots of time and are self-employed or retired, it is easy not to know how to create a structure for our creative life. For many years, I worked forty-plus hours as a teacher and business owner, so I was used to showing up on Monday morning to work. In fact, I now have anxiety on Monday mornings if I don't get something productive done. But especially if you're new to the creative life, you need to figure out a structure for working. Some work two to three hours in the morning. Some work two to three hours or more in the afternoon or evening. But if you show up at the same time every day, then the Muse knows where to find you, and even if you're not enthused about working that day, you will find yourself at your desk or in your studio moving forward.

Having a plan for our day and work helps us stay on track. Examine how you are spending your time and whether or not you need to include helpful activities to give your work juice.

Lack of Time Who does not feel the lack of time in our ever busier world? And who does not feel that time is speeding away? It's Monday, then Friday. Where did the time go? I find if I want to control time, it doesn't work. Or, if I schedule too many activities in a day, I can become frantic and begin fighting with time. But each of us is given twenty-four hours a day.

Start noticing where your time goes. Make a circle diagram representing the sixteen hours you are awake. See what activities you're doing and evaluate if you really need or like them. What can you let go of? By reducing your unnecessary activities, you will find and "make" more time.

It's also great to set boundaries with those around you. Tell them you need your writing and art-making time. It's your work. If you work at home, get up earlier or go to bed later when the house is quiet. Your work will energize you. When life is pressing against you, wanting you to give up your time, remember it's *your* time.

Life Trauma If you've been on the planet for long, you most probably have experienced trauma—whether mental, emotional, or physical. Welcome to earth school. Most of us have lived through many past lives and definitely experienced trauma. In my psychic healing practice, I am constantly removing energetic knives, axes, and swords from clients' chakras and clearing them from the effects of some horrendous past life experiences. Sometimes I am amazed people return to the planet, but they do. When you clear the trauma, whether past or present, by using the pendulum, often the talents from those lives will be released and re-enlivened. You may need a hypnotherapist, therapist, or psychic healer to help you.

Limited Idea of Self You may be living in too small of an idea of yourself. Who or what else can you become? Can you expand your creative identity?

Overwhelm You may have too much to do in too little time, and you're overcommitted. Learn to say "no." Learn to say, "I can't help you right now." I had a client who, right after a reading, called and ten minutes later wanted another question answered. I answered his question, and the next day he wanted another consultation outside of my business hours. Finally, I told him I was busy until next week. I was being drained energetically. What is draining you energetically? Identify it. Put boundaries around it. Keep those boundaries. You deserve your own space. You deserve to choose how much and how little work and pressure are right for you.

Past Life Trauma You may be carrying baggage from a past life. A hypnotherapist, Spiritual Therapy consultant, or psychic healer can help you examine your past lives and release the trauma. Often after the process is complete, new talents and skills that are needed in this life show up!

Poor Habits We all have a few poor habits. Examine which ones you can leave behind, and clean up your act.

Self-Judgment Usually, self-judgment is a negative voice that keeps us small. Examine how you truly feel about yourself, and release any outdated, false, and cumbersome ideas about yourself.

Shame When we are young, our parents, teachers, religious figures, and the culture at large use shame to control and train us. By shaming us, they teach us who to be and not be, what to say and not say, what to do and not do, and what to wear and not wear. When we are shamed, we have a feeling of being outside our family or community. But feeling shamed as an adult can knock you into a little girl or boy trance. I call them "shame attacks." They can make you feel as if you are not clean, right, or lovable, and certainly not creative or smart. You can clear yourself with your pendulum. Then call a supportive friend.

It's a paradox that to be an artist you must push against that edge of being unique and different, and that is the risk every artist takes and what makes an artist great.

Victimization Life can be difficult, and we may feel like a victim. But if we can get help through our difficulties, we can, with perseverance, turn our troubles into life lessons and gifts.

Advice

One bit of advice can open a window, a door in your mind. Take what fits and leave the rest. I asked, "What advice can you give to a creative friend?"

Find something you love and be absorbed in it.

—HAPPI CAMPBELL, sculptor and painter

I encourage you to make your passion and joy into more than a lifestyle, but a true vocation. Push the limit. Ask, how can my creativity inspire and help the world? Then go for it!

—MAGDALENA MONTAGNE, poet and poetry teacher

Don't be so hard on yourself.

—SANDRA SHAMMA, singer and songwriter

Trust your instincts first, and accept critiques as well.

—CATHERINE SEGURSON, founder of the *Catamaran Literary Reader*

Don't dig too many shallow holes.

—KRISTA POLLOCK, chef/baker

Always have fun.

—SONIA LE, fashion designer

Give yourself a deadline.

—MAHA TAITANO, sculptor and installation artist

It's important to embrace living with uncertainty. Uncertainty while working creatively is a sign you're doing things right.

—ELIZABETH MCKENZIE, novelist

Solutions Chart (10)

What works for some might not work for everyone. Different negative beliefs, distractions, and blocks call for varied solutions. That's
why there are a lot of choices on the Solutions Chart—from creating
structure to getting therapy, from playing to dancing your blues away.

Affirmations A favorite mind tool to reframe and rewrite buried negative messages or beliefs is affirmations. You simply create a new,
wiser, more wonderful thought, opposite of the negative thought,
which you cancel and clear from your mind. It's helpful to write the
affirmation in the present and include your name. "I, _____, am an
incredible artist, who breaks through into light, transformative spaces. My art communicates and opens people to visual realms. I truly
am brilliant!" Repeat until it becomes part of your consciousness.

Artist Date From Julia Cameron's book *The Artist's Way*, an "Artist
Date" in its purest form is a date you make with yourself to visit a
place you find inspiring to your work. It can be a visit to a museum,
an art gallery, or a bookstore, or it can be listening to music. What's
amazing is that, even though this is a pleasurable time, you might
run into your own resistance. Your first inclination might be to scoff
and say, "I'd feel silly being all by myself." Or a favorite, "I don't have
time." Or, "I don't like really like museums." You might forget to plan
your date. Suddenly, someone calls you and wants to talk or meet.
You might think, "I'll go later." I could come up with a hundred rea-
sons why not. But try planning and going on an "Artist Date." You will
be rewarded, and it might be one of your best dates all week.

Buy Materials Yes, you really do need better materials. Buy the best
quality materials you can afford. Your work will look much better.
It's a way to honor your work and yourself.

Clear Yourself and Your Space To clear yourself, see and check the
Clearing Needed Chart (3).

Create a Studio Yes, you need a place to play and work, whether it's
in your house or not!

Create Structure I do have a structure for my working and living
life. I take time for my morning ritual; Spirit gives me a list, and I
exercise, today, jogging three times around the Tannery Arts Lofts.

I did want to go jogging at the beach, but hey, I was really afraid I wouldn't write, so I stayed home. That was a small victory. At other times, when I am really discouraged or uninspired, I will spend more time exercising and let myself be renewed by the plants, the sound of the waves, the seagulls, and the peaceful, salty air. Afterward, I go to work for a minimum of two hours or more. I always feel better when I show up for my practice. If you wait until you are inspired, you may start but never complete your vision or project.

Dance I believe in dance. All those cells that have been sitting in the chair have to move. When you dance to music, your subconscious may offer up solutions to your work, and you will feel better physically and spiritually. You can do this all by yourself. Yes, you may feel self-conscious, but just close your eyes. Now shake, shake, shake your booty!

Do Something New Yes, do something you've wanted to do and have never done. It will wake you up and cross-pollinate your art with new ideas.

Exercise I am a huge fan of exercise, and experts agree with me too. Walking, swimming, and dancing are so good for you. Pick something you have fun doing and learn to love it.

Expand Ideas Take the idea you have and make it bigger. To brainstorm, put your idea in a circle in the center of a piece of paper. Then draw arrows from the circle to other circles. Add other ideas to your circle. When we brainstorm, we do not criticize our ideas. Just keep adding ideas. At a later time, go back to your diagram and, with your pendulum, choose seven of the best ideas. You have just stretched your idea.

Experiment When I am fearful that I won't be able to do something, I just tell myself that this is an experiment. I am not obligated to do my work perfectly. I am merely experimenting. This approach can lead you into bold, original areas of expression.

Explore Get lost and explore a new medium. Get lost and explore a new neighborhood. Get lost and find yourself.

Hire a Coach It is great to have a person who has taken the path before, someone who can keep you accountable and who is rooting for your success.

Join a Supportive Group When you have the support of other safe, well-intentioned artists and you are all focusing on a common goal to help each other improve, grow, and transform, you can do amazing things.

Journal So many ideas can slip away. You can use any method you like to remember them. The important thing is that you have a space to write your deepest thoughts, longings, and ideas. A place to vent losses and celebrate wins. It's like having a new relationship with yourself, your Muse, and your Creator.

Make Your Art a Priority At the end of the day, what is more important? That you wrote, worked on your video, painted? Or cleaned, shopped, and surfed the Internet? What is your priority? If you're working in a job or career, carve out time. In the morning before everyone gets up. In the afternoon while waiting for your child's lesson to be over. At night after you tuck everyone in. Doing your creative work will give you energy. It did when I had a company, children, a house with a yard, a dog, and two cats. What's your priority?

Meditate There are many profound ways to meditate that lead you into the inner silence. Find one that works for you. See Jack Kornfield's *Meditation for Beginners*.

Mentor Others When you give your knowledge and expertise away, you will inspire another. You too will be rewarded and inspired by them.

Play Is it time for a break from work? Or is it time to put play back into your work?

Pray Yes, there is a Creator. Call on Her for help, in large and small ways. She is waiting for your message and wants to help you.

Practice Outstanding musicians practice every day. So, should you, in one form or another, whatever your art form. Pick up the pen, the brush, or the instrument. Just practice your art with love and joy in your heart.

Practice Mindfulness Mindfulness is spiritual, being aware and alive and connected to your breath in whatever you are doing. Pay attention to the task at hand and breathe in and out. Let your worries and the busy mind go. Practice breathing in and out slowly. When your mind wanders, bring it back to whatever you are doing, whether it's art-making, driving, or standing in line (the hardest). You can practice mindfulness anywhere.

Sit in the Chair Right now I am in a chair. Some days it takes me so long to get here and to work, it's amazing. But if you receive this answer, just go to the place you work, sit, and begin. That's all you have to do.

Therapy Sometimes you do need a therapist who understands artists to help you unblock. When I joined Toastmasters years ago, I couldn't speak in front of a group, which is a requirement for Toastmasters. In a therapy session, I learned that past and present life trauma prevented me from speaking my truth. After two therapy sessions, I was so much better that I learned to speak, won ribbons, and remained in Toastmasters for eighteen years.

Experiential Exercises

Dowsing

NEGATIVE BELIEFS CHART (7)

- What negative beliefs are causing me problems right now?
- What negative beliefs are unconscious and running me?
- What negative beliefs am I holding on to so as not to proceed or work?

DISTRACTIONS CHART (8)

- What is my primary distraction?
- What are my top three distractions?
- What distractions do I need to let go of?

CREATIVE BLOCKS CHART (9)

- What is my primary block?

- What are two other things that are preventing me from creating my best work?
- What block is subtle, sneaky, that I can't see?

SOLUTIONS CHART (10)

- What solution will best help me through these negative beliefs, distractions, or blocks?
- What other solutions will help me?
- What solution(s) do I have resistance to?
- What solution(s) would ignite my work?

Practice your dowsing skills daily for a week. Keep track of your answers in your dowsing journal. What keeps showing up? What is shifting? What breakthroughs have you had?

Journaling

- What are your negative beliefs, distractions, and blocks?
- What are your solutions?
- Have you noticed your resistance to or fear of doing these exercises?
- What three solutions are you going to try to help free your consciousness?
- Write three affirmations to support you and counter any belief, distraction, or block! Post them in places you look daily. Repeat them out loud! Write them out five times in your journal.
- Were you surprised, elated when you saw a shift in the negative belief? Or when you were able to let go of your distraction? Or when the block disappeared?

Art

See Chapter 15, "Paint on Your Hands."

CHAPTER 7
Fill the Creative Well
(Charts 11–14)

When it is working, you completely go into another place;
you're tapping into things that are totally universal,
completely beyond your ego and your own self.
That's what it's all about.

—KEITH HARING, American graffiti artist and journal writer

When I am writing or painting, often I feel as if I am inside a deep well, swimming and flowing with the creative energy. I am focused and breathing, and to a greater or lesser degree, the mundane outer world fades and disappears. By filling our lives with beauty and inspiration, we are able to more easily dive deep into this sacred, fun place. We will continue to discern our desires, learn by playing, find our support team, and spark our creative lives.

Artist Needs (Chart 11)

Artists have specific requirements. When your needs are met, you can get down to the business of creating. Your work will continue to enchant and excite, and you will have a fulfilling, ever-expanding artistic life. I've listed twenty-three possible artist needs found on Chart 11. Although this list is not exhaustive, it can help you get in touch with your own requirements.

Affordable Housing Finding the perfect, reasonably priced place can take time and energy. Remember to tell the fairies your wishes and the angels your prayers, and tell them exactly what you want. Write a list, and don't forget to put affordable housing there. Keep affirming that Spirit is doing for you what you cannot do for yourself, and that all your wishes and dreams are coming true. Keep your eyes open and look for synchronicities.

Audience Creating in a vacuum is difficult. Having an appreciative audience can inspire you to innovate even more. This audience can be your dog (who will listen to all your poetry), an Artist's Way group, a writing group, or an art class. When just beginning, keep your work safe and share with positive, nontoxic people. As you learn, you don't want to be stopped by a blocked creative.

Community When you have a like-minded community around you, you have a sense of safety and security, and of being part of something greater than yourself. In today's world, this community can be online or offline.

Connection with Source When you are feeling one with the Great Creator, one with your Muse, in alignment with your goals and values, it is effortless to excel. Well, yes and no. You might have your challenging days, but if you don't quit, you'll make it to the finish line.

Daily Structure Structure will help you through the difficult times when you feel unmotivated. If you have a structure for your work and creative life, you will naturally do what needs to be done, even if in the moment, you're not enthralled with what you are making or accomplishing. You will automatically show up to your canvas, your paper, your desk, or studio.

Down Time You need time to rest, relax, and recharge.

Food Eat well and drink lots of water.

Friends Surround yourself with friends for fun, excitement, and the times when you need a shoulder to cry on.

Full-Time Work Sometimes we just need to pay the bills, and our spare time can be used for our creative work.

Fun In my creativity coaching and readings, I often tell people to have fun. It's so important to break out of the work, go play, and then come back refreshed. What is fun for you to play at? Can you do something you used to love, but left behind, like skydiving, bike riding, wind surfing, or surfing? Or drawing, painting, or playing cards?

Grants Go for it. What do you have to lose? A slim pocketbook? The only people who will receive grants are the ones who apply for them.

Income Sometimes I just ask the universe for money, an income, so that I can continue my creative work. We don't have to earn every dollar.

Part-Time Work A part-time job can provide an income if expenses are low and give us enough time to do our creative work. If you enjoy the work, even better. It will feed your life and art.

Quiet Quiet is so helpful and necessary when you're trying to focus.

Relaxation Is it time for renewal—a pedicure or spa day, time in nature, or a vacation?

Respect I always think of Aretha Franklin! I hear her voice belting out her song "Respect." No one says the word *respect* like Aretha. Once, I was feeling as though I wasn't getting the respect I deserved, so I practiced doing the six-minute exercise in the book *The Healing Code* by Alexander Loyd and Ben Johnson. Within days, I changed my beliefs and my mind, and people in my life immediately began to be more kind, loving, and respectful. A student from my Artist's Way class stood up at Toastmasters and gave a three-minute mini-talk on the benefit of my classes and said what a great teacher I was.

Solitude Do you need quiet time by yourself to start or finish that project?

Sleep Are you getting enough sleep? Are you going to bed early enough? Should you take a nap?

Studio Isn't it time you had your own space?

Tribe I love the word *tribe* because it connotes a small band of fearless warriors going forward to conquer their world.

Validation Call a trusted friend, coach, or mentor when you need validation to keep on making art.

Variety Is your routine too stultifying? Do you need a break from your schedule just for a day? Give yourself a change and then get back to your work.

Work Space Sometimes you just need a desk to get your work done. Sometimes you need a larger space to create. Ask your Guides to lead you to the right and perfect space.

Artspace

Artspace is the leading nonprofit developer of live/work artist housing, artist studios, arts centers, and arts-friendly businesses in the U.S., and I am fortunate to live and work at one of their properties—the Santa Cruz Tannery Artist Lofts. Their statistics are revealing—fifty-three properties in operation in the U.S., five properties in development, and 230 communities consulting with them (*www.artspace.org*). All of this to create affordable housing and work spaces for artists and to revitalize local culture of so many cities, such as Seattle, New Orleans, and sixteen properties in Minnesota where they first began in 1979.

The Santa Cruz Tannery Art Center and the Tannery Artist Lofts sought to preserve the history of the former Tannery upon which our campus is built, but also create a wide-open cultural space for festivals and events. As the painter Sarah Bianco said, "I've lived in Santa Cruz for a long time and there have never been this many dynamic people living in one space, . . . It makes me feel like I'm doing something valuable, not only for myself but also for the community as a whole." (*Good Times*, "What's to Come for the Tannery Arts Center," Elizabeth Limback, November 4, 2009.)

I want to give a shout out to the visionary Ceil Cirillo, who gathered and led the efforts of the Santa Cruz community to redevelop the Tannery site to assure Santa Cruz's cultural arts identity, and enlisted Artspace and numerous city, state, and federal agencies to develop the project. "She was really good at engaging and inspiring just the right people," said former Santa Cruz Mayor Cynthia Mathews, "and creating a very broad base of support. One of our great economic strengths is our creative community, and she really put it out there front and center." (Wallace Baine, "Ceil Cirillo: The Tannery Arts Center Honors Its Most Influential Figure with Art," *Santa Cruz Sentinel,* February 16, 2016; updated September 18, 2018.)

Play and Learn (Chart 12)

I love the word *play*. Children learn through playing, which helps their imagination, dexterity, and their developing minds. But somewhere along the line we forget how to play. It's so important for destressing and relaxing. "Play releases endorphins, improves brain functionality, and stimulates creativity" (see "The Importance of Play in Adulthood" at *wanderlust.com*).

When we substitute the word *play* for *work*, it immediately takes the slog and heaviness out of work.

Following are suggestions found on Chart 12 for you to enjoy yourself and learn at the same time.

Attend a Conference It was at the Santa Barbara Writers Conference where I met my first agent, made writing friends, took classes from a published author, and learned about the joys and challenges of the writing life.

Attend a Festival You can find a wealth of inspiration at a celebration. Take pictures and bring those ideas home.

Attend an Art Class Being dedicated to building your skills will help you rise to the next level in your work.

Enroll in a College Class Enrolling in a class is a bit more challenging, but why not get serious about your writing, music, or art?

Explore a New Art Medium If you're stuck in painting, how about attempting sculpture? If a musician, why not try a new instrument? Every time you explore a new medium, you will grow exponentially.

Find the Magic If you look for the special, sweet synchronicities, you can find the magic in everyday life.

Hire a Creativity Coach A creativity coach will help you expand your personal vision of yourself and what you can accomplish. You will be held accountable to another, who can help you envision and channel your passions into the creative arts.

Join an Artist's Way Class Julia Cameron's book *The Artist's Way* includes a twelve-week recovery program that has been facilitated worldwide by artists and therapists. Find one in your area or online so that the group can carry you forward. I had the book on my shelf for four years but only finished reading it and doing the exercises when I was in a group. Now, I have facilitated these groups for years, and I am still learning. It becomes a way of life. (See *juliacameronlive.com*.)

Pursue a Degree Go for it. You're worth it. Pursuing a degree should help you learn, develop skills, and possibly increase your income.

Retreat Yes, solitude on a retreat can re-enliven your work life.

Schedule a Psychic Reading Psychics have helped me understand what therapists couldn't, and they have also given me excellent advice at key turning points in my life. Ask friends to suggest a reputable one. In every profession there are charlatans who just want your money.

Take a Workshop Just a short four-week class can help you relaunch your work.

Take an Online Class I love online art classes. You can take the classes in your own home, and some allow you to go at your own pace, watch video classes, and do other activities. Two of my favorite online intuitive painting teachers are Flora Bowley at *florabowley.com* and Tracy Verdugo at *tracyverdugo.com*.

Take Bookstore Time I always feel I am visiting my friends, the authors and their books, when I go to a bookstore. Collectively, there is an amazing intelligent energy there!

Take Library Time You can take home a pile of books from the library, and the only cost is the cost of your local library card. The library can be a quiet space in the midst of a go-go life.

Travel I love being in new places. Traveling awakens my senses, makes me feel alive and adventuresome. I always visit at least one museum and, yes, a coffeehouse.

Visit Art Stores Even if I don't need anything, I just love hanging out in the aisles of art stores when I am stuck or confused or need to unwind. Many people go to bars, but I go to art stores and bookstores.

Visit Museums What a treat to see old and new paintings and sculptures in unique spaces!

Write a Life Review Writing a life review will help you get in touch with your life as a whole and help you process events, forgive yourself and others for mistakes made, and release the past. You will find gifts along the way.

Writers Adult Camp

I teach at the Catamaran Literary Conference every summer. To me, it's like adult play camp: For five days, we live in dorms on a spectacular green campus, eat delicious meals that are cooked for us, write, take field trips to literary sites, swim in an Olympic-size swimming pool, and hike through the Del Monte Forest. In the evening, we dress up; meet on the deck of a gorgeous redwood and stained-glass windowed chapel; mingle with famous writers; and then hear an inspiring talk by authors, poets, and other literary giants. Adult camp. After I return home, I always take a leap in my writing. (See *catamaranliteraryreader.com*.)

Spark Creativity Chart (13)

It's Monday morning, summer—gray, foggy, and cool—and I am staring at a blank screen, writing this little essay, "Spark Creativity." I opened to the chart and it said, "Exercise." I will go for a jog and be right back. "Ms. Muse, do you want to come with me?"

I just returned and I do feel better. While I was out, I noticed these incredible little yellow flowers among the dry summer weeds, just blooming and exuding their love. Now I'm ready to work.

Here are a few other ways to spark creativity found on Chart 13.

Be Curious Curiosity fed the cat! When you feed your inquisitiveness, you will be rewarded. You will venture into new territory, discover new land, and be nourished. Some are thirstier for knowledge than others, but if you cultivate curiosity as a habit, you will enlarge your world and your work.

Commune with the Muse Who has been visited by the Muse? Who has felt her sometimes intense and sometimes gentle pressure to start working? I never knew the Muse was real. In Greek and Roman mythology, the Muses were nine goddesses, the daughters of Zeus and Mnemosyne, who presided over the arts and sciences.

My Muse's name is Cleo, and now she and I have a more conscious relationship. I always attempt to do what she is asking. Because the results are so good, I feel better when I work with her, and my work shines! When I began painting, she would not leave me alone for nine months. Later, when I was writing my book *Catching You, Catching Me, Catching Fire*, which also took nine months, she whispered in my ear. Now when She comes, I am so grateful!

How do you ask the Muse for help? Just like you would ask a friend. You can write to her in your journal, ask in your mind, or say it out loud: "Help, help!"

Dream Go for the biggest and best, and you can touch your inner greatness. I've had a number of high-tech creatives in my Artist's Way classes over the years. One told me that when he had a vexing problem, he would write it out, put it on his nightstand, and let go. In the morning, he somehow always had an answer.

Embrace the Dark "Creativity, like human life itself, begins in darkness," says Julia Cameron. As a child, I was always afraid of the dark, but now I find pleasure in it. When we don't know and are in the dark, we ask questions. Being in the question allows you to open your mind before you find your answer.

Embrace Your Sexuality You got it. Use the force for good and creativity.

Find Humor We need to find the humor when everything is at its bleakest. You've heard of gallows humor?

Find Joy Even in the darkest days, look for the flowers and blessings.

Have Faith "In Spirit All Things Are Possible" is my faith mantra. I have the saying on my dresser, where I see it every morning. Faith is funny. You would like it when you need it most, but it can slip away. If you can't summon it, remember the mustard seed parable? Jesus said, "The Kingdom of Heaven is like a grain of mustard seed, which a man took, and sowed in his field; which indeed is smaller than all seeds. But when it is grown, it is greater than the herbs, and becomes a tree, so that the birds of the air come and lodge in its branches" (Matt. 13:31–32, King James Version). If you're unfamiliar with this famous parable, research it online or in books.

Honor Nature Honor nature, in the physical world and in yourself, of which you are a part of the plan.

Honor the Child Within Our creative self is a child. Very precious, precocious, a little bratty, and lots of fun. If you've never met her consciously, ask her what she wants. You'll be surprised at the answers you get. Sometimes I have to tell her, if we finish the page, then we can go out and play. Sometimes, I just let go and let her lead the way.

Listen To or Play Music I always wished I could play an instrument or sing, but second best is exploring music and what helps you to be creative. Is it rock 'n' roll or classical, hip-hop or rap that you love? If you are one of the gifted ones who can play an instrument, pull it out and play to the gods.

Look for Synchronicities Another wonderful intuitive habit is to observe and expect uncanny coincidences—or what Carl Jung called synchronicities—almost like waking dreams. They are mini-miracles, where everything on the physical is aligned; you find just the right source for projects, you run into people you thought of but forgot to call. You have the feeling of being guided, protected, and loved. You may make a wish for art or writing supplies internally and not even express it out loud, and presto, there they are.

Meditate Breathe and find your inner silence. There are many paths to our inner being.

Paint Yes, you can paint. You can find the joy in the brush, the colors, as they flow on the paper.

Play Go ahead and play! Just for fun!

Practice Gratitude Practicing gratitude, if you make it into a daily habit, can turn your life around. By practicing appreciation and giving thanks for what you have, you can see from a different perspective and improve your reality.

Practice Intimacy Let yourself love and be loved by others. Just notice if you get uncomfortable. And breathe.

Praise Birds and Animals When you pay attention to the variety, the color, the shapes, and qualities of birds and animals, you enhance your life. In the morning, I bird-watch from my window. In the afternoon, I walk to meet all the dogs on the path. They cheer me up. Even though I don't have my own dog, I can make friends. They always have a wag and a smile for me.

Praise Plants and Trees I live five miles from Henry Cowell Redwoods State Park, home to ancient redwood trees. Whenever I want to commune with trees, I go there and walk along the San Lorenzo River that leads to the Redwood Grove. And yes, I do hug them.

Praise Earth, Sky, Oceans, and Rivers By praising, you are joining in creation. The earth, sky, oceans, and rivers enjoy your appreciation and honor.

Wonder Wonder is a quality of being open with your heart and mind to experience the mystery of being alive in a phenomenal universe.

Support Team (Chart 14)

Who is on your personal support team? Who is backing you up? Encouraging you? Use your pendulum on Chart 14 to access this information.

Agent An agent can connect you with publishers or galleries, review contracts, and urge you to write your next book or begin your next work of art.

Angels I've worked with my angels of light and love for twenty years now. You can begin a relationship with them simply by asking for their help. They do not interfere with our lives, but when we ask for their guidance and assistance, they will be there with their practical advice and gentle wisdom.

Archangels Archangels are the all-embracing, higher-level angels who can assist with larger issues: Gabriel helps with communication, Michael with protection, Raphael with healing, and Uriel with wisdom. When they appear in client readings, I am always amazed by their size, power, and love.

Coach A creativity coach gives you the time to gain clarity on your goals, mission, purpose, and message and helps you develop a plan for taking action. A coach can hold you accountable to that plan and help you envision next steps. You will feel empowered to go further and deeper in your work.

Creator I love the name Creator for God because it reminds me that our God is the most amazing, stupendous creator of all. He/She does not stop at creating one bird or flower or plant or tree, but thousands, millions. Our Creator wants us to not only create but to also create abundantly!

Diviner/Dowser I am a diviner/dowser! Are you? This is a person who uses a rod or pendulum to elicit intuitive and sub- and super-conscious information that is not readily apparent to the conscious mind.

Editor An editor helps you review, revise, and improve your writing.

Family Member My sisters have helped me more than any other people on the planet.

Friend Mark Twain said, "Good friends, good books, and a sleepy conscience: this is the ideal life."

God In monotheistic religions such as the Christian religion, God is seen as the Supreme Being.

Goddess The Goddess is seen as a Supreme Being of female essence.

Great Spirit This Native American name for God/Goddess encompasses the courage, strength, and fortitude Spirit can share with us.

Higher Power This name for God/Goddess is used in twelve-step groups.

Mentor You may already have mentors, such as book authors you've never met or artists whose paintings you have seen only in galleries or museums. Or you may be lucky enough to have experienced and trusted advisors in your working life.

Minister Sometimes you need spiritual counsel and help.

Muse The Muse can be so elusive at times, but so powerful. Invite Her into your creative life.

Psychic *Psychic* has two definitions: (1) relating to or denoting faculties or phenomena that are apparently inexplicable by natural laws, especially involving telepathy or clairvoyance; (2) relating to the soul or mind.

Significant Other Even he or she can help you. Sometimes you need a hug, a talk, an intimate partner's guidance and love.

Sponsor In twelve-step programs we have sponsors who guide us in the program and who, at times, save our lives.

Teacher "It was my teacher's genius, her quick sympathy, her loving tact which made the first years of my education so beautiful. It was because she seized the right moment to impart knowledge that made it so pleasant and acceptable to me." —Helen Keller from her book, *The Story of My Life*.

Therapist A therapist is helpful when we are stuck or have deep emotions that need expression. My last therapist was a great listener, and my life turned around while working with her. *Don't be afraid to ask for help!*

Experiential Exercises

Dowsing

ARTIST NEEDS CHART (11)

- What do I need right now?
- What will I need in the near future?
- What do I need to further my work?

PLAY AND LEARN CHART (12)

- How could I play today, this week?
- What would lighten me up?
- What do I want to do right now?
- What would enhance my creativity?

SPARK CREATIVITY CHART (13)

- What do I need right now to spark my creativity?
- What am I not seeing that could help?
- What am I resistant to?
- What else could help?

SUPPORT TEAM CHART (14)

- Who is helping me right now?
- Who can help me on this project?
- What other type of support would help me?
- Whose advice do I need to seek?

Journaling

- Write a wish list (ten to twenty-five wishes) to fulfill all your needs.
- Put your wish list in a Prayer and Wish Box where you keep all your special wishes and prayers. Write three affirmations related to your wishes and fulfilled needs. See them as already appearing in your life. You can say them out loud to give them energy. Now post them where you can see them.

Art

See Chapter 15, "Paint on Your Hands."

CHAPTER 8

Discover Your Creative Identity and New Art Directions

(Charts 15–20)

The value of identity, of course, is that so often with it comes purpose.

—RICHARD GRANT, British author, journalist, and TV host

In our teens and twenties, and for many of us in our thirties and beyond, we are attempting to discover answers to the questions "Who are we?" and "What is our work in the world?" Parents, friends, and schools attempt to steer us in the right direction to help us find our way, but if we don't know who we are and our purpose, it's difficult to know what our next steps are and how to make a contribution to this ever complex, highly specialized world.

Some souls are fortunate to know at an early age, "I'm an artist!"— like my daughter, Danielle. Or her best friend, Gwen, who knew she wanted to be a doctor and studied, worked hard, and became a physician. Or my friend Will, who became an engineer and built bridges all over the world. People like Danielle, Gwen, and Will have a fairly direct educational path, and some will have a job and career waiting for them right out of college.

But what about the rest of us? In middle school, it's not easy to be different, so if you survive that *and* high school while still being yourself and an authentic being, you will find yourself in a new world needing just your kind of unique. Jacob Nordby, in his book *Blessed Are the Weird,* says, "The only success now is living and creating a work-of-art life: unique, rich with meaning . . . " Coincidentally, a slogan for my little town is "Keep Santa Cruz Weird."

The issue of making a living while becoming proficient and skilled in the arts has led some dedicated writers, painters, and creatives to work part-time or full-time in other jobs or professions. They work on their art in the early morning, late at night, and on weekends.

That approach certainly is true for most of the artists at the Tannery Artist Lofts, where I live and work. Joseph LaCour is a poet, author, and spoken word artist who lives next door; he holds a job as a delivery person all over the Bay Area. He works on his poems in his head while he drives the long miles. Sarah Bianco, an incredible fine art painter and muralist, paints houses for a living, while maintaining her art studio at the Tannery and making murals all over Santa Cruz.

I like the idea of finding work in the world that can support you, perhaps even enliven your creative work, and *pay you well.* For instance, many artists become teachers, like myself. I teach a few small classes, and I not only teach but also learn from my students.

Perhaps you can find a job in any profession that doesn't sap your energy or spirit, so you have plenty of time for creative interests. Did you know that the poet Wallace Stevens spent most of his adult life working as an executive for an insurance agency? And William Carlos Williams was a doctor of pediatrics and general medicine?

Cheryl Strayed of *Wild* fame says in *Brave Enough: A Mini Instruction Manual for the Soul,* "YOU don't have to get a job that makes others feel comfortable about what they perceive as your success. You don't have to explain what you plan to do with your life. You don't have to justify your education by demonstrating its financial rewards. . . ."

Okay, the mom in me with two grown adult children who are both artistic wants to answer back, "But, but, I want you to have an easy life. A home, a good income, security. I want you to end up with the material goodies, a title (Wow, where did that come from?), and a lot of money in the bank. Don't do what I did—leave my career to pursue the arts! Are you crazy?"

Elizabeth Gilbert, author of *Eat, Pray, Love*, says, "Wisdom does not come from age, wisdom comes from doing things."

So, go out in the world and do as much as you can. Don't listen to your mom or your dad. Make that video. Star in that movie. Sing on that stage. Write that song, that poem, that symphony, that play, that book. Do not let anything stop you. Go on, show me what you can do.

From a Knowledge-Based to a Creative Economy

As technology replaces many human work arenas, creatively working is more important than ever. Mark McGuinness, author, blogger, and creativity coach, explains that we are transforming from a knowledge-based economy to a "creative economy." He cites John Howkins, author of the book *The Creative Economy*, who states that thirty-eight million Americans or 30 percent of all employees are creating new ideas, technology, or creative content. His notion of this new group of people is broad, and includes scientists and engineers, as well as designers, educators, and artists. McGuinness also cites Richard Florida, author of *The Rise of the Creative Class*. His thesis reveals how relevant the topic of creativity is and how important the arts are to our global society as a whole (see "The Rise of the Creative Economy," *lateralaction.com*).

The National Endowment for the Arts corroborates these findings: "The arts contribute $763.6 billion to the U.S. economy, more than agriculture, transportation, or warehousing. The arts employ 4.9 million workers across the country with earnings of more than $370 billion" (*www.arts.gov*).

A headline from John LaRosa on February 12, 2018, proclaims "U.S. Personal Coaching Industry Tops $1 Billion and Growing" (*blog .marketresearch.com*). So coaching and creativity coaching will continue to expand and grow.

In a world asking for the new, the different, the *avant-garde*, we are seeing that creative people are being rewarded.

Creative Identity (Chart 15)

If you really have your own identity, you'll keep on doing what you think is really right for you, and you'll also understand the next step you want to take.

—HELMUT LANG, fashion designer

If you've wondered what you might excel in and don't know yet, please dowse the next Creative Identity Chart (15) and then explore hobbies, vocations, or careers with the Digital Arts (16), Home Arts (17), Literary Arts (18), Performing Arts (19), and Visual Arts (20) Charts. You might discover through them that you have a wide range of potential playgrounds to explore and thrive in. Open your heart and mind. "Life is a daring adventure or nothing at all," said Helen Keller.

The gift of creativity is that your unique self brings your inquisitive mind, heart, and soul to your work. The "Other" category on this chart exists because there are infinite possibilities of who you are and who you could become.

Who Am I? What Is My Role in Life?
Who Will I Be? What Profession Will I Find?

When I started college, I didn't know what I wanted to be when I grew up and ended up fascinated by anthropology and archaeology. At home, I began studying spirituality and the psychic arts through books and tarot cards. After receiving my BA, I enrolled in a credential program and became a teacher in San Francisco, California, and Sao Paulo, Brazil.

In my mid-thirties, I began working as a contractor at Apple Computer; there I discovered I had a knack for business, marketing, and publishing. I had much to learn, but at Apple everyone had much to learn. All personal computer technology and writing, painting, graphics, photography, and publishing software were brand new. I had just said yes and done the next right (or at times wrong) thing. Every day I learned so much on the job. It was a challenging but thrilling time for me. Even though Apple had gone through a big upheaval at that time (1986), the creative energy was palpable and vibrant.

In my mid-fifties, I realized that the intense stress from running my company was impacting my health. After September 11, 2001, and another economic recession, I gradually lost the motivation to lead my marketing company. It was during this time I declared out loud, "I want to be a writer." Not until my late forties and early fifties, when I became a spiritual consultant, a psychic healer, writer, painter, and creativity coach, did I feel I had finally found my rightful, ever-evolving place in life.

Digital Arts (Chart 16)

What we're doing here will send a giant ripple
through the universe.

—STEVE JOBS, Founder of Apple Inc.

In 1977, Steve Jobs and Steve Wozniak launched Apple and their first computer, Apple I. In 1986, I began working at Apple. I felt like such a neophyte, and I had only taken two short computer courses while introducing computers to teachers. The Macintosh Plus, with its floppy disk drive and laser printer, was brand new. Luckily, Apple offered courses for employees and contractors to learn programs, such as Word and Excel, and later, the all-new graphics programs. My first logo for the company I founded, JointSolutions Marketing, was created in MacPaint and the stationery in MacWrite. I was fortunate to be at Apple as desktop publishing and the digital arts took off. Artists in all genres now use technology in multiple ways to generate original creations, run their businesses, and market their work. The digital arts greatly expanded our artistic toolbox from the traditional to the electronic and made it possible to reach an expanded audience worldwide.

Some of the skills and arenas in the vast digital field include:

- **Animation**—creates visual effects and brings characters and settings to life.
- **Cinematography**—manages the camera crew, controls and directs all shots or camera movement on set.
- **Directing**—manages the crew, actors, and other personnel.
- **Environmental Modeling**—brings settings to life. It's helpful to have a graphics design, architecture, and interior design background.
- **Game Design**—creates themes, rulebooks, and establishes characters and the plot of games.
- **Graphic Design**—combines artistic and technological skills to create visual concepts that communicate ideas.
- **Illustration**—draws and creates original pictures.
- **Multimedia**—uses mixed media such as film, video, and computers to create special effects, animation, or other visual images for use in products or creations such as computer games, movies, music videos, and commercials.
- **Photography**—captures and preserves images. Today's photographers have technical expertise with digital cameras, lighting equipment, and editing software.
- **Videography**—films or tapes, edits, and produces videos.
- **Web Design**—creates a website for a client, including overall look and feel, as well as functionality and features.

Home Arts (Chart 17)

Life isn't about finding yourself.
Life is about creating yourself.

—GEORGE BERNARD SHAW

Home arts can bring us great joy at any age. In a mechanized world where machines make most products, homemade baby blankets and clothes, furniture, pottery, and especially food can bring a soulful, rich feeling into our lives. Making things with our hands can connect and reconnect us to our self-sufficient and creative selves. Check out this pleasurable chart that will help you find how to enhance your being and life with home arts. This is a way to use your creativity in both a practical and artistic way. What are the home arts that express who you are?

How I Was into Home Arts in My Twenties . . .

In 1971, I married early—I was just nineteen. Now, I think that is an early age to get married, but back then I had a lot of pressure from my parents. They kicked me out of the house for not getting a summer job (my mother was going a little nuts due to financial pressure), then disowned me for "living in sin" with my boyfriend. I was in between my first and second year at San Francisco State University, a few miles away from where the "flower children" of Haight-Ashbury started their peace and love revolution. We lived in Albany, California, next to the University of California, Berkeley, home of the "Free Speech Movement" and anti-war protests against the U.S. involvement in Vietnam. Our high school friends were being drafted into that illegal war.

But what was I doing? I wore a long, empire-waisted, purple, cotton dress, sandals, and was learning how to bake bread from scratch, cook brown rice casseroles, and make the best drip coffee in world. We had a mini-commune at the Albany one-bedroom house, mattresses on the floor, and even an active beagle named Millie, the chubby runt of the litter. We opened a little store called "Allofus" on Solano Avenue that specialized in handmade pottery, macramé plant holders, stuffed animals for children, and small psychedelic paintings for peering at when you dropped acid. My boyfriend, Art, was older, with a law degree from UC Berkeley School of Law. He opened a law office in the back room that paid the rent for the store and the house. Thank you, Art!

On the front porch of our little house, my girlfriend Peggy and I learned how to embroider patches on our boyfriends' and our scruffy jeans and made "Winnie the Pooh" stuffed animals for the store and ran the store, which really meant opening it, vacuuming, and waiting for customers who usually never ventured that far down Solano Avenue to our little enterprise. That summer, we read Aldous Huxley's *Island* and Robert Heinlein's *Stranger in a Strange Land.*

Later that year—with much pressure from my mom and dad—I married Art, and the following summer, we ended up in hot Stockton, California, where I painted the whole interior in 100-degree-plus heat, sewed curtains, learned to can strawberries and peach chutney, and hosted dinner parties for my now-husband's law partners and their wives. Later, I learned to knit, crochet, and quilt while we watched the long-lasting *Star Trek* series with Captain James T. Kirk (William Shatner) and First Officer and Science Officer Spock (Leonard Nimoy). It was a happy life. I was only twenty-one.

It wasn't until the COVID pandemic this year that I sewed and mended again. Anxiety is helpful in getting all those little projects done. My daughter, Danielle, was impressed I could hem a dress by hand and that my stitches were even. I still bake chocolate chip cookies and blueberry scones, cook homemade chicken soup, and make the best coffee in the world.

Literary Arts (Chart 18)

In the beginning was the word.

—JOHN 1:1, King James Version

I was fortunate to grow up in a house filled with built-in library bookshelves lining the walls from floor to ceiling. One of my earliest memories is my mother taking us to the library to pick out our weekly pile of books, and by thirteen, I became an avid reader of the classics. When I was in eighth grade, an eccentric, older teacher introduced us to Charles Dickens and Jane Austen. It was almost as if I had two lives: My ordinary waking teen self was interested in clothes, makeup, girlfriends, and yes, boys! The other self was a young woman who read the classics and modern literature often late into the night. I had a secret life!

Since the beginning of time, people have told stories to pass on knowledge, history, and wisdom. Stories help us survive, thrive, and give meaning to our lives. "Stories are important, the monster said. They can be more important than anything. If they carry the truth," says Patrick Ness, author of *A Monster Calls*.

Words are such a part of our human consciousness; we can take them and our literary world for granted. Speaking and writing are such gifts we have, and how wondrous that, with a few words, we can transform life. Martin Luther King Jr. gave his most famous speech, "I Have a Dream," on the steps of the Lincoln Memorial on August 28, 1963. Today, over fifty-five years later, his words are still reverberating, and we are still being transformed.

There is something enchanting about words and books. As Isabel Allende says, "The library is inhabited by spirits that come out of the pages at night." We've all felt the power of the word when poems, song lyrics, and stories wake us up, move us, and often transport us to another time and place.

Words survive beyond the human life span. As E. B. White said, "People have managed to stay alive by hiding between the covers of a book." Words transform our minds and souls and guide us, whether through a poem, parable, or story.

Now, years later, I teach, facilitate, and volunteer for a literary publication—the *Catamaran Literary Reader*, which is published at the Tannery Arts Studios. (See *catamaranliteraryreader.com*.) The quarterly journal is a rich, brilliant magazine full of poems, stories, and essays, plus visual arts from West Coast artists. After publication, we gather to celebrate (in person and online) its release into the world, listening to the voices of the poets and storytellers.

You also have the opportunity to join this literary world, simply by being a reader, a listener, or a writer yourself. Check out your local library and bookstore for stimulating books; attend in-person readings where you will learn authors are real, live human beings; journal in your morning pages; or join a writing class. You don't have to tell anyone. Yes, it can be your secret life. If you're looking at this chart, wondering "Could I be a writer?" you most probably are.

Use the Literary Arts Chart (17) to discover what you are curious about, what you are drawn to, where your talent lies, and what might be your next literary adventures.

Performing Arts (Chart 19)

To kick off National Dance Week in April, Motion Pacific, a local dance studio, holds an event called "Santa Cruz Dance Week." On three stages for three hours in the late afternoon each day of the week, the streets are cordoned off, and there are forty-nine plus performances, ten minutes each, to give all the dance and movement groups time to strut their stuff. Children of all ages in colorful costumes take the stage and wow us. Older tango couples show us their elegance, grace, and sensuality.

When I was new to town, I hadn't heard about the event. As I exited Bookshop Santa Cruz downtown, I ran into the performers and the large circles of parents and spectators gathering around. I had the feeling that I was in a musical, where dancing and melodies had invaded our town—complete with little ballet dancers in pink tutus, hula dancers in straw skirts, and flashy ballroom dancers. Around the corner, there was another stage with African, Tahitian, Brazilian, and Latin dancing; and another, a block away, with aerial performances.

Simultaneously, seventy-five communities across the United States were celebrating Dance Week. To top it off, Flash Motion Mobs popped up to entertain us spontaneously over the weekend. In Santa Cruz, free classes in dance and fitness are offered all week long.

In a world where we view so much on a screen, in-person live events help reinvigorate you—whether you are a participant or part of the audience. Every performer needs enthusiastic spectators. As novelist Ann Patchett says, "Some people are born to make great art and others are born to appreciate it. Don't you think? It is a kind of talent in itself, to be an audience, whether you are the spectator in the gallery or you are listening to the voice of the world's greatest soprano. Not everyone can be the artist. There have to be those who witness the art, who love and appreciate what they have been privileged to see."

I can't wait until the Coronavirus leaves town, our state, our great nation, so we can seriously get back to celebrating and living out loud.

Visual Arts (Chart 20)

Not until I began painting intuitively did I see "art."
Pick up that paintbrush . . .

When I began painting spontaneously and intuitively, art was no longer on a wall or in a museum. Art was inside of me wanting to express itself through my being. While I painted, I experienced a calm, focused feeling, where my busy mind was quiet, and I heard a new silence as I painted. I couldn't wait to wake up in the morning and see what Spirit would paint through me.

Since then, I have taken classes at Cabrillo, my local community college, which was building a new art department and has an excellent faculty. There, I took drawing, color and design, and watercolor classes where I was more formally introduced to the arts. As part of the training, students had to visit local art galleries, museums, and venues such as coffeehouses and art movie houses, and report back on at least twelve different art experiences in a semester.

In the spring of 2019, I had a short visit to Van Gogh's museum in Amsterdam and saw multiple floors filled with his work. One thing you notice about his work is that it is full of feeling, imagination, rhythm, and life. His story of spiritual searching, painting, and mental illness has made me feel that, despite all human trials, we can rise above and celebrate our humanness. Van Gogh made little money from his precious, inspired work, yet he left us a most priceless collection of paintings.

Am I Really Creative?

In my last Artist's Way class in spring 2020 (that was in person for the first six weeks and virtual for the last six weeks), all of us were still questioning whether or not we were truly creative and whether or not we were artists. Susan was an architect/interior designer from New York, Jean was a painter and sculptor from New Mexico and Mexico, Kathy was a healer/aromatherapist starting a new online business doing Facebook live events, and Linda was a painter and children's book author. Every week we created new projects to warm up artistically.

Artists often do not think of themselves as real artists! Not artists with a capital *A*. I think it has to do with how all of us are so unique. One art form is not like another, and each artist has their own talent, skills, and process. In my Artist's Way class, we practiced saying the words out loud—"I'm an artist. I'm a writer. I'm a musician, a singer-songwriter."—to stand up to our own minds and confirm our identity.

Experiential Exercises

Dowsing

CREATIVE IDENTITY CHART (15)

- Who am I today?
- Who do I want to become?
- What is my creative identity today?
- What other profession would guide me in the right direction?
- What is surprising me?
- What don't I want my conscious self to know?

DIGITAL ARTS CHART (16)

- What would I like to explore in the digital arts arena?
- What would be fun to learn?
- What is surprising me?

HOME ARTS CHART (17)

- What home arts do I love?
- What home arts express who I am?
- What type of home arts would be good for me?
- What type of home arts would be good for my soul?
- What else could I learn to do that would be fun for me?

LITERARY ARTS CHART (18)

- What do I love to read?
- What do I love to create?
- Where does my talent lie?
- Where does my interest lie?
- What would be good for me in the future?
- What genre would help me expand my literary career?
- Is there any area I should focus on right now?

PERFORMING ARTS CHART (19)

- What types of performances do I enjoy seeing? Hearing? Performing?
- What type of show did I participate in as a child?
- What type of music lessons did I have?
- What would I consider as a vocation? As a career?
- What brings my heart, my soul alive?

VISUAL ARTS CHART (20)

- What kind of visual arts would I excel in?
- What type of visual arts can I explore?

- What can I play in?
- Where does my talent lie?
- What is my hidden talent?
- What visual art would cross-pollinate my primary work?

Journaling

- Who do you want to be when you grow up?
- What is your creative identity?
- What "titles" and "creativity identity" are you comfortable with?
- List five things you created in your childhood. List five things you've created in your adulthood. Are you a creative?
- List five ideas of things you would like to create (for instance, a cake, a song, a poem, a collage . . .). Give yourself permission to stretch the idea of who you think you are. Set a challenge outside your comfort zone and grow into it!

Art

See Chapter 15, "Paint on Your Hands."

CHAPTER 9

Use Conscious Creative Processes and Tools

(Charts 21–24)

One must still have chaos in oneself to be able to give birth to a dancing star.

—FRIEDRICH NIETZSCHE, German philosopher and writer

What is your creative process? Some of us turtle along, others zip, some of us are cheerful morning people, others night owls. Some of us have a plan and know exactly what we're doing and where we're going, and others intuit their path forward one step at a time. But one thing all successful artists have in common, whether consciously or not, is that they have a process that works just for them.

If your current method doesn't seem to be flowing, use the Creative Process Chart (21) to see where you're stuck or need a boost and the Principles of Design Chart (22) to remind you what you most probably already know within but now can be more cognizant of when examining your process and work. For visual artists, I created the Color Chart (23), and for writers, I included an Elements of Story and Writing Chart (24) to help you examine, edit, and revise your words, poems, stories, songs, and books. I ask the forgiveness of dancers, musicians, and other creatives for not including specific charts for you. However, I included thoughts and ideas from of other artists and their processes in this chapter (see sidebars).

Creative Process (Chart 21)

I was especially grateful to a writing teacher, Barbara Bloom, who pointed out, "That's your creative process." She was referring to my method for putting together a writing project. She helped me realize I needed time between drafts, time to reflect, time for research and writing, and time for revision.

I hadn't focused on the term *creative process* until I picked up the inspiring book *Fearless Creating* by world-renowned coach Eric Maisel, author of over forty books. In *Fearless Creating's* 300-plus pages, he offers a step-by-step process for starting and completing your art. The process included on my chart is slightly different, but I learned much from Eric Maisel.

Then there is that word *process*, which always tells me that this idea or project is going to take time. Lots of time, and it's not going to happen in an instant, overnight, or even in a month. So slow down, breathe, and buckle down for a longer ride.

The Creative Process Chart (21) will help you quickly know where you are in your progression. Why does that help? Why is it needed? It's like having a map, knowing where you are, how many more miles up the mountain you have to hike, and also, that you are on track. Each part of the course has its own challenges, and this chart will help you cross each crevice or boulder when you come to it.

I just asked, "Where am I in the process of writing *The Creative Pendulum*?" It said, "Deep Middle to End," "Daily Work," and "Share with the World." It surprised me, but I did give a virtual talk this summer on "Spark and Sustain Your Creativity," which is another section and chart in this book.

Thirteen categories are included on the Creative Process Chart (21).

Inspiration Inspiration is an underlying feeling that something is coming, that a project wanting your attention is suddenly calling to you. Sometimes you might not know what it is, but when you are in this phase, it's great to dialogue with the Creative Spirit in your journal and ask, "What is my next project? What do you want me to focus on? What project is for the highest good of all?" Also, talk to friends or a mentor and express your ideas and feelings. Sometimes, in ruminating out loud, ideas will pop out of your mouth. Write them down! You can also research ideas and thoughts using the pendulum and charts, asking the question, "What is my deepest desire to create right now? Again, write them down. Ideas can be slippery.

Dreaming Sometimes our best ideas come through dreams. To get insights into your projects, write down questions in your journal before you go to sleep. Ask that you be shown symbols and signs in synchronistic ways, either in sleeping, meditating, or waking. Live with your questions, "What is my soul's deepest desire?" Ask that the highest and best next project be revealed to you.

Researching Some projects require much research—for instance, a historical novel. Perhaps you must not only do the library work but also must visit the setting of your novel. Perhaps you need to find out all about the culture, art, food, colors, plants, animals, and sounds and smells of that distant time and place. Or you need to investigate the music of that period so your book has a certain rhythmic quality that matches the chronology of your novel. For work set in current times, perhaps you need to meet and interview people who can give you original source materials. Other projects require much less research. Or you may need to start and then do research periodically throughout the writing process. But do not get caught in the sea of other people's work and forget your own work. Write, paint, produce, sit in the chair, face the expanse of white paper or canvas, and enjoy!

Planning You've found your project! This is an exciting moment. Now this is the phase I love. Take the time to hold, ponder, and think deeply about your work to come. Write down your thoughts, draw, or collage your ideas, activating all parts of your brain; then brainstorm your project on a flowchart. Ask the Creative Spirit to keep the ideas coming and add to your notes, outline, or diagrams. After finishing the planning phase, you can dowse to determine your best ideas. Which ideas can help you to further your plan and figure out the big steps? See the Intuitive Action Plan Chart (32).

Gathering Materials What do you have, and what do you need? Do you need new art supplies? A new computer? New dance shoes? What other resources will you need? Make a list of materials— whether or not you think you can afford them. You can then ask the Creative Spirit to bring all you need and more. Affirm: *Spirit is bringing to me all I need and want. Thank you, Spirit, for all that I have and will receive.* Be on the lookout for those supplies or money coming to you in usual and unusual ways.

I have a girlfriend, Amy, who was in my Artist's Way class. She was especially adept at manifesting very specific items. Once, another woman in the class wanted red cowboy boots, and presto, the next week Amy brought the boots to class. She literally had found them a block away from her house on the sidewalk in a "free" box. "Ask, and it shall be given you; seek, and ye shall find; knock, and it shall be opened unto you" (Matt. 7:7, King James Version). Sometimes, though, you have to be patient. I am always telling this to myself. The angels are always whispering in my ear, "Be patient." For me, that's the difficult part. I have places to go and places to be, and the current manifestation is not matching my dreams. But there is a mystery about timing. After years of cocreating with Spirit, I know that when something doesn't appear easily and quickly, there is a higher reason. Positive forces are aligning for all the necessary and next steps on the never-ending journey. When I have been patient, I have been given much more than I ever thought possible, and the unfolding plan is even better than my own.

Committing Now you're ready to commit to your project. After all, you will be spending a great deal of energy on this endeavor. Ask: Is the project worthy of your time and effort? Is it something you will want to work on for a length of time?

I was taken aback when looking through my file cabinet: I found a partial beginning of *The Creative Pendulum* from fourteen years earlier. When I saw the date, I was surprised that so much time had passed, but then I took it as a sign that I had to proceed and complete this book. I believe now is the right time. I must admit that I have gathered spiritual and artistic wisdom in the ensuing fourteen years.

Create a simple ritual for yourself and your new project. Write down all hopes, dreams, and wishes for the project. Add a statement of commitment that you have written or use the following one:

> *I offer myself to the Creative Spirit and Muse. Bless*
> *and enliven and bring this project into the world. I*
> *ask for your clarity, brilliance, and divine assistance*
> *to flow through me, and to be a channel for your love,*
> *light, and genius.*

Then practice a little candle magic. You can light any candle you love, or choose a blue one for commitment, red for the fire of action, or gold for all the wealth and wisdom your project is going to bring into the world. Read your commitment statement out loud to yourself and perhaps a trusted friend . . . and your Creative Spirit . . . and your Muse. Afterward, put your commitment statement into your prayer box!

Beginning At last, after preparing for the journey, you're ready to embark on your great adventure. Your energy is high; you're happy—and sometimes exalted! You're fully prepared. What could stop you now? Beware of anything or anyone who has a more tantalizing idea, project, or even a job. It seems that resistance is greatest at the beginning and end of all projects. Keep your focus and carry on. After all, you made a commitment to your original creative work.

Deep Middle to End Sometimes, in the middle, our energy wanes. We seem to have entered a dry patch and can't find the water. Be sure to continue your morning quiet time practice to fill the well, and remember to ask for guidance in your journal. If you get weary, bored, and things are not making sense, show up for your project anyway. You're committed. You can review your dreams, wishes, and commitment statement from your prayer box. Write another prayer and listen for answers.

At the same time, this period can be a joyous experience and the most satisfying part of the journey. You are now in tune with your project, and it's speaking to you. As you work, you are learning, growing in knowledge, attempting the impossible, and climbing that mountain! Work every day, do not take excessive time off, or you will lose that momentum. This is a sacred time, when you and your Muse are cocreating together.

Reviewing After finishing a day's work, a week's work, step back and take a break. Let the project rest. Then review your work with fresh eyes. I like to review work after a good night's sleep. Remember to view your work with compassion. No, it's not finished yet, but even in its awkward stages, you don't harshly criticize. Like you do with a preteen or teenager who goes through a time of great bodily changes, complete with acne and braces, you just give that child love and reassure her that she is beautiful.

Revising Writers sometimes do twenty drafts of their work. Ask for help from qualified people. This is a good time to enlist a trusted teacher, creativity coach, writing group member, fellow student, or editor to assist in reviewing your book.

Completing Ask the question, "Is this project complete for now?" As Eric Maisel reports from his years of creativity coaching, some things are complete for now, but at a later stage, we might go back and rework or revise.

What does complete feel like? It's funny. I'll share my secret. When I do a bit of prose writing or write a poem, I have an inner feeling of completeness, and then I hear, "Amen." Then I say, "Ah-women." My little God/Goddess joke. You might have a similar inner signal.

When I was painting, I would hear very loud and clear, "Stop!" Sometimes I would and sometimes I wouldn't listen, but later I would always regret that I hadn't stopped when prompted to do so.

You can also dowse with your pendulum to ask and receive a *yes/ no* answer:

- Am I complete for right now?
- Am I ready for a break?
- Is it the right time to stop?
- Is this layer on the painting complete?
- Is this painting/poem/song complete?
- Is anything missing that I cannot see?
- Have I forgotten anything?
- Is it time to stop for the morning, the day?

Review your original idea and compare it with what you attempted to accomplish. Yes, the work, while creating it, will have transformed, but have you embodied the unique and wonderful qualities that you set out to? Have you reached the top of your personal mountain?

Share with a Support Group First, share with safe members of your creative circle—safe sisters without jealousy, brothers who share your passion, writers who are on a similar path, and artists who like your work and understand it. Safe, meaning the group you choose will enhance, not destroy, your poem or painting. Safe, meaning if you feel sad or disheartened after a writing group, and, with reflection, you do not feel supported, then find a new group of safe creatives. Only you can decide who will help you clearly see your project and offer constructive ideas before you release it into the bigger world. I am fortunate; my poetry teacher Magdalena Montagne is a great coach and editor. She always says, "I can't wait to see your next chapter," because she believes in me and my work. I return to my desk, my little studio office, and write for her and my other friends and readers who appreciate me.

Sharing with the World Now it's the big time, and you're ready to let your creative work into the world. You have invented this amazing, unique being—whether a book, a song, a painting—and now you must let it stand on its own and find its own way in the world.

In my morning quiet time at this stage, I envision my project being escorted by angels and my project itself with wings, arriving in the divine right time to the perfect people who will benefit from my book. I see my book courageously and with great resilience making its way to special bookstores in every town and state, and worldwide. Spend five minutes daily for seven days envisioning your project warmly received and with gratitude. (I just heard that little "amen," telling me that you, dear reader, understand.)

Over the years, I've seen myself pick up clues from both fellow and well-known writers. We all have our own way of entering our work, engaging, flowing, and completing. When you find and recognize your own process—special time, place, and way of entering the magic door—honor, thank, and bless it; do not let it go until you are complete for that moment, that day, and that project.

Creative Process

I asked my circle of fellow artists, "What is your creative process?" I loved their input and am passing it along to you.

Energy in motion.

—RACHEL VAN DESSEL, painter and dance teacher

I find that I'm most inspired to create in nature. The outdoors, from the ocean to the mountains, generate so much productive energy for me that I then return home and capture or translate via my computer, notebook, or other instrument of expression.

—JOSEPH LACOUR, spoken word poet, artist, and emcee

Sometimes, I have to wait for an idea to take form. In the meantime, I can be in nature painting watercolor sketches or practicing my music instruments—in search of beauty. Ideas take form, but I move rather slowly.

—HAPPI CAMPBELL, sculptor and painter

I find the quiet, light candles, drink tea, and put on music to help the creative flow.

—CATHERINE SEGURSON, founder of the *Catamaran Literary Reader*

I usually don't have a plan to start a piece. I start and the process and mistakes lead me on.

—MARIA CHOMENTOWSKI, visual artist

I don't have a formal sequence, but sometimes I do ten minutes of meditation and then declutter my desk area, which winds up taking too long. I listen to soothing or classical music.

—PAMELA PAPAS, writer and stand-up comedian

There are two aspects of my creative process. The first is the conceptual, an inner dialogue I have with myself. The shower is my best intellectual brainstorming office for narrowing my concept and deciding what I want to produce. The second part of the process is thinking of how many elements there are, breaking the pieces down into steps, creating a timeline, and guidelines of how and when I'm going to produce this. I create in multiples, so there is a long, laborious crafting that happens. I enjoy watching myself become this art machine, and my studio an art factory.

—MAHA TAITANO, sculptor and installation artist

Every time I start something new it's like starting from square one. I'm groping in the dark. I move forward step-by-step, deciding where to go based on unexpected developments along the way. Usually, a string of good days is followed by a few bad ones, which I now have learned to expect.

—ELIZABETH MCKENZIE, novelist

I work with oil paint and collage on canvas. I begin with material exploration, with layering of textures and images. Messiness and chance often play a large role in my work. I layer and scrape, add a dab here, or tear off a piece here. My process is very intuitive. Color, architecture, texture, and the interior of my body are all things that I think about while I work.

—DANI TORVIK, artist

As a pastry chef/baker, my creative process is tossing yummy and amazing ingredients together . . . throwing all of them in the oven . . . crossing my fingers and hoping for the best. Then, later scribbling new notes over old notes in my very sticky and tattered recipe book. Do this a million times and you will finally have your perfect, go-to recipe.

—KRISTA POLLOCK, chef/baker

I look to others who have wisdom to guide me. William Stafford, when asked how he could write a poem each morning, said he "lowered his expectations." I rely on my students for inspiration—to listen to all those just-birthed poems is like being present as a newborn enters the world—quite remarkable (and humbling). Insights also come from my reading. Going back to those poets who comfort and astound me with each read, and finding new voices as well. Learning something new generates original ideas, and then assimilating these into poems, borrowing from another lexicon. Ernest Hemingway said, "All you have to do is write one true sentence. Write the truest sentence that you know."

—MAGDALENA MONTAGNE, poet and poetry teacher

Design Principles (Chart 22)

The Design Principles are not just a way in which to analyze your work and projects, but also a way to live your life. As humans, we need balance and movement, rhythm and repetition, white space (down time), and variety. When you learn these principles, you begin to see them everywhere.

I was just out for my morning "power jog but now walk" as my girlfriend calls it, and noticed how the Tannery Artist Lofts embody many of these principles—balance, hierarchy, contrast, proportion, repetition. The Tannery Artist Lofts were designed to honor the past site of an actual working, leather-producing tannery that played a key economic role in our city. Also, to ensure that working artists had a place to live, to guarantee the future of the arts in Santa Cruz.

The language of design and these principles were created to work together to aesthetically communicate the artist's vision. Examine your own work and discover the principles already present. You will find the following principles identified on Chart 22.

Balance The way in which the visual weight of objects, colors, texture, and space are shared in a space.

Contrast The juxtaposition of opposing elements such as color, value, direction, or texture to create a dynamic feeling of life.

Emphasis The way one area of a painting stands out through the use of contrast in size, shape, color, or texture.

Harmony A combination of similar related elements such as colors and shapes.

Hierarchy (or Dominance) Emphasis given to some elements to give a painting visual interest, counteracting disorder and repetitiveness.

Movement The path taken through the viewer's eye through a piece of art. For instance, oblique lines suggest action.

Pattern Repetition of an item or symbol through the work of art.

Proportion All parts relating well with each other.

Repetition Replication that makes the piece seem active and helps unify a painting, poem, or song.

Rhythm The pattern that is created when one or more elements are used repeatedly to create a mood or feeling.

Unity The relationship between items that links the various parts of a painting with a feeling of harmony between all parts of the work, which creates a sense of wholeness.

Variety A set of various items that spark the viewer's attention and creates interest.

White Space The negative space that is left unmarked on a page or canvas.

Design Elements

Design elements are a set of guidelines for graphic artists and are the basic units in any visual arts piece. This is a simple list for your beginning arts education:

○ Line—Linear marks of all sizes and variations that connect or separate objects.

○ Shape—A self-contained area made with a line.

○ Size—Scale and proportion of an object in relationship to another object.

○ Texture—Surface quality of a shape or painting.

○ Color—See Chart 23.

○ Value—How light or dark it is or isn't.

Color (Chart 23)

At the West Coast Dowsing Conference, I took a class on color healing that helped me understand the restorative power of color: Yellow can help sadness and depression; red is for energizing and empowering; blue is for calming, communication, and expansion. Then, when I began intuitive painting with Golden acrylic paints, I truly fell in love with color. Painting with yellow lifts my spirits; turquoise connects me with the Great Creator; and pink, red, and magenta help invigorate me.

I noticed that after painting intensely and being in a deep space for a few hours with various colors, it would be like traveling from an inner space back into "normal" consciousness. The colors outside and in nature appeared much more vivid, and I began seeing flowers, plants, birds, the sky, ocean, and beach in brilliant hues. Even while driving and walking, I'd notice the color of buildings, signs, and what people were wearing. I also began wearing colors based on my activities for the day.

Flora Bowley, in her vibrant book *Brave Intuitive Painting*, reminds us that you don't have to know everything about color before beginning a painting. She writes, "It's better if you don't. I hope this relieves any worries, such as which colors to use and how to combine them. Let those questions dissolve and consider that every color is an opportunity." As you use pastels or colored pencils or paint with watercolors, acrylics, or oils, you will be drawn to certain colors and want to experiment with them, and you will notice that your color choices and palettes will naturally evolve and transform.

In art classes at Cabrillo College, I was introduced to the color wheel and color mixing. It was a little overwhelming to me, but I was glad I had already formed relationships with color before learning anything about color theory.

Did you know that Sir Isaac Newton (in 1703) created the color wheel based on the colors representing the visible spectrum of light?

There are primary colors—red, yellow, and blue; they cannot be mixed or formed by any other combination of colors. Secondary colors—orange, green, and violet—are hues (a color or shade) derived from mixing of the primary colors.

Color mixing still feels magical—how you can take yellow and red, and create orange; yellow and blue to make green; and blue and red to make violet. If you have never done this, you should stop right now and play with the primary colors and make these three secondary colors.

Seven Colors of the Rainbow

What are the seven colors of the rainbow? Red, orange, yellow, green, blue, indigo, and violet (which are also the colors of the chakras!). The acronym "ROY G. BIV" helps you remember the color sequence.

Twelve Colors That Appear on Basic Color Wheels

- **Primary colors**—Red, blue, and yellow.
- **Secondary colors**—Orange, green, and violet.
- **Tertiary colors**—Those colors created by mixing two secondary colors in between two primary colors: yellow-orange, red-orange, red-purple, blue-purple, blue-green, and yellow-green.

You can make your own color wheels, buy them at an art supply store, or download them from the Internet.

A Few More Terms

- **Complementary colors**—Colors opposite of each other on the color wheel, these create a high contrast and vibrant look; for example, red and green, blue and orange, and yellow and violet.
- **Analogous colors**—Colors next to each other on the color wheel that create serene and comfortable designs and are often found in nature; for example, red, orange, and yellow; green, blue, and violet; and yellow, yellow green, and green.

- **Color triads**—Color evenly spaced around the color wheel—red, yellow, and blue.

- **Warm colors**—Red, yellow, and orange.

- **Cool colors**—Blue, green, and purple.

- **Neutral colors**—White, black, and gray.

The hues on the Color Chart (23) include the primary and secondary colors, the neutrals (white, gray, and black), three metallic colors (silver, gold, and bronze), plus my favorite colors (pink, purple, and teal). You can add your favorites to the chart also.

• Black	• Orange	• Teal
• Blue	• Other	• Violet
• Bronze	• Pink	• White
• Gold	• Purple	• Yellow
• Green	• Red	
• Gray	• Silver	

A unique way to choose colors for your project is with your pendulum. You can choose just one color or create a palette. Especially if you don't know the next color to use, you can dowse the Color Chart (23) to help you decide. You can ask if your painting needs one color or more. Then try mixing those colors. Or you can dowse your paint tubes directly and see what works. It's fun to paint with your pendulum assisting you.

Elements of Story and Writing (Chart 24)

Making Chart 24 was cool because I knew I would use it to assist me in writing this book and in my other work. Sometimes, as writers, we get lost in the middle of a piece. Use your pendulum with the chart, and you will be guided.

The Elements of Story and Writing Chart (24) is to help writers primarily in the editing stages after laying down a first draft on paper. Storytelling elements are also included, as these are used in fiction and nonfiction, as well as poetry. The following elements are found on Chart 24.

Antagonist An adversary, someone who is in conflict with the protagonist of a story.

Brevity Keep it short, especially in poetry, but this is also true in any skillful writing. As William Shakespeare said, "Brevity is the soul of wit."

Characters The people who populate novels, plays, or movies have different roles and purposes to play in the story.

Clarity Often the most difficult part is to say exactly what you mean to say and say it clearly.

Conflict As in life, clashing characters give books spark and vibrancy. We all love mysteries, and life seems to be about finding out who did it, how it happens, and where. Even in love stories, sometimes characters must draw guns to make the reader engrossed in the story. Remember *Mr. and Mrs. Smith,* the movie with Brad Pitt and Angelina Jolie?

Dialogue Dialogue brings the reader directly into the story, reveals character, and makes a story come alive. Do you remember the dialogue of Master Sergeant Farell (played by Bill Paxton) in the film *Edge of Tomorrow*? Farell said, "It's a new day, people! Destiny calls. The world expects only one thing from us: that we will win!" just before his parachute opens out. Later, when Cage (played by Tom Cruise) watches soldiers being slaughtered and then runs from the gunfire, Farell admonishes, "Now then, Cage! You're going the wrong way! You're going to miss your moment!"

Grammar Oh, yes, we hated it in elementary school. Yet when writing uses common language and rules, the reader can easily decipher the writer's meaning.

Message What are you truly attempting to communicate? Clarify and rewrite.

Metaphor This figure of speech states one thing is another thing, for comparison and symbolism.

Narrator This can be a character in a novel who tells the story from a first-person viewpoint.

Narrative Arc Without an arc to the story, we are left feeling, "What's the point?" The five chronological plot parts are exposition, rising action, climax, falling action, and resolution.

Outline An outline includes topic, purpose, main ideas, and points in a hierarchical sequence.

Point of View Who is telling the story and from what point of view?

- **First person**—The character is fully in the story.
- **Second person**—The storyline is told to "you."
- **Third person**—The narrator is outside the story, or omniscient— with full access to all characters' thoughts and experiences.

For further information, see the Point of View Guide at *thewritepractice.com*.

Punctuation Fourteen different marks are used in English to separate and clarify.

Plot The sequence of events in a story form the plot.

Protagonist The leading character or hero in the story is the protagonist.

Purpose The big "why" or goal of why we are writing is to express, provide information, persuade, or create an artistic work. When writers know why they are writing, they will be able to convey and communicate more easily with their readers.

Rhythm Can you hear the beat? Rhythm is a strong, repeated pattern of movement or sound in music, poetry, and writing.

Setting The time and place of a literary piece define the setting.

Similes These figures of speech compare one thing with another, usually using *as* or *like*.

Structure The organization of a piece of art or writing creates its structure.

Theme This is the underlying subject or topic of a piece of writing.

Unity The parts of the whole piece fit together and add a sense of harmony and focus to your writing.

Variety The quality of being different or diverse adds that special chili to your writing.

Word Choice Is there a more descriptive word?

Experiential Exercises

Dowsing

CREATIVE PROCESS CHART (21)

- Where am I in my creative process?
- What do I need to focus on?
- Where am I stuck?
- What area of the process do I need to revisit?
- What can help me move forward? (Start at the Table of Charts and ask to be guided to the right chart.)

PRINCIPLES OF DESIGN CHART (22)

- What is the one element that would improve my paintings? (See the "Design Elements" sidebar. Dowse the list and see what comes up.)
- What could be a guiding principle for my art?
- What else does my artwork need?
- What can I focus on to improve my art?

COLOR CHART (23)

- What are the colors I am comfortable painting with?
- What colors could I add to create a calmer feeling?
- What colors could I add to my palette to enliven my painting?
- What colors could I add to create contrast?
- What colors could I mix together for a new hue?
- What would work in this drawing? Painting? Mural?

ELEMENTS OF STORY AND WRITING CHART (24)

- What's working in my writing?
- What aspect of writing do I need to focus on?
- What is not working?
- How could I improve my writing?

Journaling

- What is your creative process? Attempt to outline how you create your best work.
- What do you notice about your creative process now that you are more conscious of it?
- Are you more aware of color in your own space, in nature, and in the world?
- What do you think about color? What colors are you attracted to?
- Is it time for a new palette? A new life?

Art

See Chapter 15, "Paint on Your Hands."

CHAPTER 10

Venture into the Business of Art

(Charts 25–26)

Being good in business is the most fascinating kind of art.
Making money is art and working is art and
good business is the best art.

—ANDY WARHOL, American artist

One of the most inspired and, perhaps, most difficult actions you will ever undertake is to step up and create your own business. Yes, rewarding and challenging, but you will learn much. If it is your true heart's desire and you are motivated, you can start a business, create income streams, and develop your own creative enterprise to fit your lifestyle. Instead of working for someone else, you can use your Spirit-given skills and talents to envision, open, manage, and establish an amazing enterprise.

This chapter is the place to begin if you are new to commerce. It offers two charts that will help you with the business side of your art enterprise. Know this is just a beginning. The Business of Art Chart (25) will help you start thinking about the needs of your business.

The Income Streams Chart (26) will offer suggestions as to how your company can develop multiple complementary ongoing income tributaries to sustain your organization.

In one way or another I have been self-employed for thirty-plus years, which, looking back, surprises me. I did lean on my Higher Power, angels, Muses, friends and family, employees, and contractors to support my children and me. I did take a "real" job or contract here and there, but primarily, Spirit guided and led me on the entreprencurial journey. If I can do it, so can you!

Some, including beginning artists, would like to hand the business and marketing of art products over to someone else—an assistant, agent, accountant, attorney, or a marketing guru. They might think: "Who, me? Now I have to become a businessperson?" Well, yes, until you have enough money to hire people who are better than you at their jobs, and who will greatly add to your bottom line, it's good to learn how to run the business end of your artistic endeavor.

In this new offline and online art world, much is expected of us—not only to create, but to run a business and market ourselves. Today, when you get a publishing deal, publishers want to know what you are going to do to market and sell your book. They want you to already have an audience and a social media platform.

When you are just beginning and are a one-person shop, you may have to consult with professionals but also do most of the legwork yourself. On the upside, the more you know about business, marketing, and *your money*, the more likely you are to reach your financial goals, make a healthy income, and succeed.

If you're like me—an idealistic liberal arts major—you probably didn't ever take a business class in high school or college. You might even have looked down at those people who handled plans, marketing, numbers, money, balance sheets, taxes, and other such mundane and sometimes frightening issues related to business life.

But now as I am older and wiser (now I'm laughing), I wish I had taken a business class or two so that I could have had a sense of the big economic picture and could have avoided the errors I made. I wish I had more academic knowledge in some practical areas, such as budgeting, financial planning, human resources, and asset creation, that might have helped me to avoid the pitfalls that every new business owner encounters—artist or not. But I gathered much along the way through magazines, books, classes, and online research.

Initially, I was worried that a business would take me away from my spiritual life, but something else happened instead. To stay centered, increase my work hours, learn about business, marketing, and new software programs—to juggle new and unique balls in the air—I had to double down on my spiritual practices, open up to new ways of thinking and creating, and let go so Spirit could work through me.

Years ago, in the dot-com era of the late 1990s, I saw and heard a remarkable slide presentation at a business start-up conference where a physician/business owner correlated the accidents his emergency room patients had and the common business mistakes they were prone to make. One actual photograph from his presentation remains in my mind—someone who arrived in his emergency room with an arrow shot through his head. Yes, the patient lived. And yes, metaphorically, I've taken my share of arrows and, though wounded, learned from them!

I want this chapter to encourage, not overwhelm, even if it's difficult for you as an artist to delve into commerce. If you ponder it— creative entrepreneurs have many skills and advantages—we spend hours in imaginative worlds, venturing into the unknown, and forging clear, powerful paths for others to follow. What we need to do is harness that ingenious power for our business ventures.

Keep Asking Spirit for Help—Look for the Gifts and Opportunities

When I started JointSolutions Marketing in 1986, I was fortunate. Now, this may sound different, but before I started my business, I spent a year asking God/Goddess for my right, perfect place, opportunity, and company. I lived in a Victorian mini-mansion, a spiritual household of former Ananda members (followers of Yogananda) in the quaint, vibrant town of Nevada City. I meditated and chanted daily, jogged, took yoga and massage classes, and swam in the nearby Yuba River. In other words, I practiced letting go that hot summer and into the fall and winter. I did not know at the time, or even later, that Steve Jobs was on a similar spiritual path studying Kriya yoga and the teachings of Yogananda through his book, *The Autobiography of a Yogi.*

Envisioning and letting go to a Higher Power can be your first step in business creation, and you can apply it to your whole life. Do your spiritual work and ask Spirit, the Great Creator, God/Goddess daily for Her intention for you. Ask Her to show you next steps. Ask for the willingness to do the difficult. Ask for inspiration and the power to do all that has been asked of you!

That spring, after praying and meditating, I began my company with the help of my sister and landed my first project. My sister had already started her own software company while she worked at Apple. She had business moxie and experience, and taught me much. In my first two years in business with my husband, James, we completed projects, rented offices, hired employees and contractors, and made enough money to buy a small house and a new car. It all happened very fast, but the late 1980s were a time of transition and opportunity in the Silicon Valley.

Years later, on the other side, in hard, difficult times, during the 2000 dot-com bust and the 2001–2002 recession after 9/11, I downsized my company from twelve to six employees and cut our office space in half to survive. Then in 2002, I transitioned again to become a consultant with contractors. I had started and continued working on my first book, *Divination & Action.* I actually wrote down what I had learned over the first fourteen years of founding and running JointSolutions Marketing and working with innovative companies such as Apple, Adobe, Oracle, and Novell, and their thousands of partners.

I knew the earth underneath my feet had shifted. I didn't want to lose the knowledge I had gained when I ran a company and wanted to share and inspire other open-minded entrepreneurs. Also, when you go through uncontrollable economic upheavals, such as 9/11 or the COVID-19 pandemic, which had and has thrown the United States into an economic downspin, you need to help your company, employees, and yourself survive a financially shattering situation. At the same time, you're trying to emotionally mitigate the effects of losing what you have worked for over days, months, and years.

If you can turn your losses into wins, especially in your own mind, and find the gifts in the turmoil and transformation, *and* keep showing up for your life and dreams, eventually the tide will turn and you'll be in a new sea of possibility. It's probably the most difficult thing to do, but as spiritual beings having a real, live human experience, the act of drying ourselves off and asking "What's next?" is the secret technique to surviving, and later, thriving. Consider also that those other dreams that have been sitting on the sidelines, tapping their toes, waiting impatiently, are calling you. Perhaps, this roller-coaster ride is all a part of the divine plan after all?

I have a deep admiration for creative business owners, entrepreneurs, small start-ups and, of course, artists who put their talents out there in the larger world. I wish success for everyone's right livelihood. Who are you not to be smart and hard working? Who are you not to be brilliant and wise? With the Great Creator's help, be the builder of your own destiny.

The Business of Art Chart (25): How to Start a Creative Business

The Business of Art Chart is a beginner's how-to-start-a-creative-company chart—a basic and simple guide to help you first think about your business and then set up the nuts-and-bolts infrastructure. I encourage you to—ready or not—take the leap into your own future.

You may want to see yourself in a brighter light with a new mindset—as an entrepreneur with passion, imagination, and a desire for sharing your ideas and products. Doesn't that sound like you? Inventive, inspired, and a hard worker?

The sooner you embrace this new business mindset—that you not only are a creative but also are an entrepreneur—the more quickly your dreams will manifest. Aren't we all about changing and transforming our lives and others'? We do this by offering our exceptional products and services.

That word *entrepreneur* intimidated me at first. Could I be that? Then it was verified. Years later I was featured in *Entrepreneur* magazine for our fun KittyCam website that my JointSolutions Marketing company employees had created, complete with a product line of T-shirts, cups, mouse pads, and sweatshirts for those dedicated fans who came to our website to see the cat. Animal websites were new, and the show *Animal Planet* even featured our ordinary black cat.

Setting up the infrastructure for a single-person sole proprietorship is amazingly easy. (A sole proprietorship means "an unincorporated business owned and run by one individual with no distinction between the business and you, the owner." See *www.sba.gov.*)

I scanned three books about how to open a business, paid for a business license, rented a mailbox, filled out forms for a fictitious business name statement and resale license, and opened a bank account, all in three days, as I was under pressure to start an upcoming new project.

The two essential must-haves to make your enterprise a success are you and your brilliant ideas . . . plus a computer to handle your business, marketing, and communications. Then, take care of the legal requirements in your city, county, and state to operate a business.

Practical words of advice: Attempt to spend as little money as possible in the start-up phase to receive the best value for your precious start-up capital. Look also for occasions to trade services, find used equipment, and take advantage of free resources in your community and on the web. Be lean and mean!

As you step up to creating your company, you will, at the same time, be learning much about yourself, facing your fears, letting go of old beliefs, and affirming a new self and mindset. Take all the spiritual and prosperity tools you've learned and draw on them to create your business. Implement those values you hold dear, and treat your employees and customers as you would like to be treated. This will be a practical spiritual journey all of its own.

On the Business of Art Chart (25), you will find what you will eventually need for starting a business.

Bank Account (Friendly to Small Business) Take your fictitious business name statement to the bank and open a checking account. Keeping your personal and business money separate is more professional and makes it easier to see and monitor your cash flow.

Budget Create a financial plan and budget for one month, six months, and a year so that you have an idea of how much you will need every month for the first year. Then, monthly and quarterly, check your real-time money flow against your budget. See and know where your money is going. Many businesses fail in the first year, all due to companies not having enough financial flow their first year. *Rule #1 in business: Do not run out of money!*

Business License Find out at your city offices whether you need to have a license. Sometimes, if you live in unincorporated areas, a license is not necessary.

Business Name Spend time brainstorming with clever wordsmiths in your friend or professional circles, as this will become a primary asset of your company. If chosen well, your business name will attract customers and concisely say what you do and sell.

Consultations with the Pros (Insurance Agents, Accountants, and Lawyers) Ideally, you would have the money and time to find the best professional services in your city or county, and you would receive excellent business advice. If you are successful in your enterprise, at some point you will need help. My criteria for choosing the best professionals are that they are (a) smart and strategic; (b) helpful (they solve your problems); (c) timely; and (d) offer mutual respect. When I began JointSolutions Marketing, some men looked down on me because I was new in the business and a woman. Not all attorneys or accountants are created equal and specialize in small or creative businesses. Their fees will be high. Do not be intimidated, do your own homework on the web concerning your accounting or legal issues, know what your questions are, and look for reviews of their services. After all, it's your precious time and money.

Desk, Computer, and Printer You can start with your own personal equipment. Upgrade as you need it.

Fictitious Business Name After you choose the name of your company, you need to file fictitious business name forms at your local county offices; some are online or offline for your sole proprietorship. Afterward, you must publish your fictitious business name in your local newspaper to make it official and become eligible for a bank account.

Fulfillment Services Having an abundance of projects, contracts, or orders can be exciting, but make sure you keep timely promises to your customers. Always attempt to give customers more than you promised and perhaps surprise them. In this era, we are all competing with companies such as Amazon that have excellent fulfillment departments.

Internet Shop around to find the best and fastest Internet connection so that you can work faster and not go crazy while waiting for a page to load.

Mailbox You need a mailbox, especially if you have a home business. A mail service such as a local UPS store will provide you with an address and will make your business appear more professional. Also, it's nice to separate your mail and give yourself a little privacy in return.

Marketing See Marketing Chart (27) detailed in Chapter 11. Start with a business card so you can begin handing out your name and services to potential clients. As you develop your company, you will need to think about company branding, a mission/vision statement, web presence, social media, and advertising. See *vistaprint.com* and *moo.com* for reasonably priced business cards and printed marketing materials.

Office Your office can be in a corner of your bedroom, a room in your house, a garage (this is how Apple began), a studio, or an actual office (often this comes later after the dollars start rolling in).

Resale License Applying for a resale license is easy but can become more complicated when reporting sales and sales taxes. I recommend talking to a professional bookkeeper or accountant.

Social Media See Social Media Chart (31).

Website Your website can initially be a one-page, do-it-yourself brochure at *GoDaddy.com* or another online web provider. You will have to buy a website address that matches your company name and is easy to find when customers are searching for what you offer.

❖ ❖ ❖

Finally, it's imperative to celebrate the little and big victories along the way. Celebrate when you have your office set up and your logo and website created. Pay attention when you make your biggest sale ever, when you make your customers happy, or when you begin marketing your services and products. You are going to have ups and downs in business—it's part of the game—but if you commemorate the important wins along the way, you will increase your joy and suffer the losses more easily. And if you learn from your mishaps and take them in stride gracefully, you will continue to grow personally and professionally.

You can read business and marketing books and research online. There are classes at your local community college, talks and workshops at your local Chamber of Commerce or the Small Business Administration, and online marketing courses for starting up a company. Also, see the following books to further your desire and knowledge to be an entrepreneur and start a business:

> *The Creative Entrepreneur* by Lisa Sonora Beam
> *Creatrix* by Lucy H. Pearce

Income Streams Chart (26)

The old motto "build it and they will come" was immortalized in the 1989 movie *Field of Dreams* with Kevin Costner. It's wise to examine the flip side of the equation—"build multiple income streams and money will continue to flow." Build your baseball field, but check in with your customers' needs. Be open to new financial and creative opportunities. It's important to diversify, so if one stream dries up, you will have other means to support your work and life.

If you are in a job that doesn't fit your lifestyle or that you dislike, start investigating other means of support and income streams. Bottom line—a boring, stressful, or difficult job with little intrinsic reward and long hours with a terrible commute can lead to the slow death of your creative self. Yes, it might take time to transition, but in the long run, you can find your right and perfect place in life that complements your creativity.

As artists, we are fortunate to be able to see a challenge from many angles and to use our imagination and creativity to build our own future. I created the following Income Streams Chart (26) with suggestions to help expand your ideas and playing field.

Audio/Video Recordings The audio book market grew by 25 percent in 2020 and is becoming increasingly more creative (see the article about the rise of books you don't read at *www.bbc.com*). And the digital video recording markets continue to grow worldwide.

Bundling Bundle your own products or bundle with a like product to sell more and add value for your customers.

Coaching Others like yourself need clarity, guidance, and support to help them on their creative path. They often need assistance from starting with the white space of paper or canvas, in the soggy middle when the path seems lost, to the too-terrifying end. Will they fall off the end of the earth if they finish their project? If you're a people person, have practical experience, and enjoy supporting others, why not think about becoming a creativity coach?

Commissions A client hires an artist to create artwork that more specifically fits the client's needs.

Consulting Up your expertise and prices, bid on projects, and be paid well as a consultant.

Contests All sorts of writing and art contests abound. Search online for grants at *pw.org* and art competitions at *mymodernmet.com*. Winning contests is helpful for your resume, marketing exposure, and your creative ego!

Digital Sales If you can create an e-version of a work, there is no reason you can't sell it online to a wider audience. Digital sales of books, music, workshops, and classes are growing.

Freelance Work Consider also freelance work for which you are paid per hour or per contract for a project.

Grants These awards are to be used for development of an organization, business, or individual and do not have to be paid back.

Job You receive a salary—a big benefit!

Licenses A license is a business arrangement in which one company gives another company permission to use intellectual property and/or to manufacture its product for a specified time for a percentage of revenue or a fee.

Online Business There are currently 7.1 million online retailers in the world, and 1.8 million of them are in the United States (*etailinsights.com*).

Other New ways to increase your revenue streams are always opening up. Say *yes*!

Performances Theater, music, and speaking events enliven our world and deepen community and cultural ties.

Prints/Cards/Clothing Prints, cards, or clothing can be manufactured through an abundance of online companies that use your art to create new product lines.

Produce Other's Work Become a publisher, manufacturer, designer, desktop publisher, videographer, or ghost writer for other creatives.

Products Products include books, crafts, art, CDs, DVDs, and so on to sell in your own shop; at conferences, fairs, or festivals; in person or online.

Royalties A publisher will pay a writer a fee for every reproducible product sold.

Scholarships Getting a scholarship for school, workshops, and conferences is a double win because you not only learn but also are honored when you're chosen for the award.

Services If you've gotten this far, you have learned much. You have skills and services you can offer others. See *What Color Is Your Parachute* by Richard Bolles to help you inventory saleable talents and skills. (Ten million copies and sold in twenty-eight languages. What an inspiration!)

Teach You have much to give others, and your students have much to teach you. It can be a win/win to inspire others and be delighted in return.

Stay open to new opportunities. Say *yes* before *no* and be willing to expand!

Experiential Exercises

Dowsing

BUSINESS OF ART CHART (25)

- Where do I begin?
- What should I focus on?
- What does my business need right now?
- What else would be helpful?

INCOME STREAMS CHART (26)

- What income stream would produce the most money?
- What income stream(s) can I add to my financial flow?
- What other income stream can I add in the future?

Journaling

- Have you ever thought of yourself as not only a creative but also as a businessperson? Why or why not?
- What do you love about the business aspects of creating? What do you dislike?
- What income stream would you like to have? What other stream?
- Can you stretch yourself and include another stream of money?

Art

See Chapter 15, "Paint on Your Hands."

CHAPTER 11

Out into the World

Market Your Art
(Charts 27–31)

Hustling—in other words, engaging with people and making things happen—is your job.

—MARK MCGUINNESS, author, blogger, and creativity coach

Marketing my books, art, classes, and spiritual counseling services does not come naturally to me. To be honest, I'd much rather be creating than "hustling" as Mark McGuinness urges us to do. I'd just like sales to happen easily, quickly, and with little effort on my part. But I must be realistic.

The irony is that I had a marketing company, but it was marketing in a print and in-person world and it was promoting other companies' products. Yes, I learned much, but still that kind of work is poles apart from presenting yourself and your image out into the world. Not to mention offering your books, art, music, videos, and other products and services out onto the global stage—the Internet. Just now, I hear my better angels, the ones always spurring me on, saying "Get over it; just do it and enjoy. Relax and make it fun." I will take that advice.

Yes, you have created an outstanding, innovative product or offer a superb service, but you must also promote and market your services (whether online or in person), and meet and greet or engage with your customers at events, stores, or galleries. It's about being in the right time and place when there is a hunger and a need for your services and product. When you mix vision, passion, hard work, and opportunity, your online marketing can grow more slowly, evolving, as has been the case for me, or exploding and going viral. See how you can use your spontaneity, originality, and imagination to pursue marketing and selling your products.

If you envision marketing as a great way to meet and make new friends who will desperately need and appreciate your product or service, it will be easier to reach out either in person or on the web. Look also for mentors who have created great books, websites, blogs, and marketing strategies that truly interest you. Spend time searching for community, like minds, marketplaces—those people and places you resonate with. If you dislike or are repelled by groups, do not go there. Attempt to find online and offline who your customers will be and engage with them. See this approach as "friendship marketing"—treating people you meet offline and online as new potential allies and friends.

The following five arenas will help you explore your business and entrepreneurial side: Marketing Chart (27), Audience Chart (28), Target Location Chart (29), Sales Venues Chart (30), and Social Media Chart (31). Your success will depend on persevering, discovering your niche, and embracing both the traditional and new digital marketplace.

Marketing (Chart 27)

Marketing is an umbrella term that can embrace a wide range of presale activities, from branding, product packaging, and messaging to excite, inform, and educate with the aim of creating a deep desire in your customers to buy your product. Today (especially during the COVID-19 pandemic), this is primarily done through online marketing websites, blogs, YouTube, or other social media platforms.

This process can be a bit overwhelming at first, but if you start with one essential marketing element at a time, such as a Facebook page or website, and add elements step-by-step, you will be amazed at how much you accomplish over time. I will walk you through and introduce you to each part, but you will have to further explore online and through books and classes, and make yourself the expert in marketing your own work. Later, when you have the money, you will outsource this effort to others, but for now, it's your baby.

Another tip: First, identify your customers' pains or needs. Then, explain explicitly how your products and service will help alleviate suffering or fulfill their needs. Realize they are searching for your offerings. Remember that your purpose, your big why, is to help and enrich them.

Advertising Paid messaging is found in all media—publications, television, or search engines, such as Google, or social media, such as Facebook.

Agent This person represents you and your work, and negotiates details of contracts.

Blogging These short and to-the-point mini-articles detail your expertise and are a good way to build an online following.

Book Writing a book can help add to your "expert" persona because it can be used as a marketing tool, whether in a printed, digital, or audio format.

Branding This marketing practice is about creating a distinct, overall product or service "look and feel" design that is easily recognizable to customers.

Brochure In specific situations, brochures can quickly help customers understand what your services are and what you are selling.

Business Card Create a high-quality, intriguing, and readable card for your potential clients.

Designer Use a designer for help with your logo, business card, brochure, product packaging, and overall look for your website and social media. A great designer will elevate everything you do and help you visually express who you are and what products you sell in the world.

DVD This medium is good for offering on the spot to people or at shows.

Email List MailChimp offers free online services and grows with your list.

Intuitive Action Plan See the Intuitive Action Plan Chart (32) in Chapter 12.

Marketing Consultant Do your homework in selecting a marketing consultant. Ask for their client list and for recommendations from their previous or ongoing clients. In this day and age, they should have a strong knowledge of social media and online sales.

Marketing Pitch A pitch is preformulated, succinct sales language to inform, persuade, and sell your product. See "6 Types of Sales Pitches Every Salesperson Should Know" at *blog.hubspot.com* for further information.

Marketing Plan A good plan can detail who your customers are, what needs you are fulfilling, who your competition is, what the marketplace opportunities look like, how you are going to present your products to the marketplace, and how you are going to make sales. You can use the Intuitive Action Plan Chart (32) as an outline for your plan.

Messaging This is an idea advertisers want to communicate to their customers to help them buy products or services.

Postcards Postcards are handy for introducing yourself (a mini-brochure) and announcing events.

Press Release Online press release services can send your press release to multiple channels, both locally and globally, to your target markets.

Public Relations Consultant Find the right PR consultant with strong contacts with all types of media companies that are relevant to your products or services.

Radio/TV Look for free opportunities to talk about your work and upcoming events.

Samples People love free!

Social Media Facebook, Instagram, Twitter, and YouTube are a world unto itself. See the Social Media Chart (31). This form of communication is necessary and great for all creatives.

Story You are going to be asked multiple times about your company and your products. Write a positive narrative about your art, books, music, and life.

Video A short visual presentation can quickly capture and tell your product's or company's story.

Website From a brochure to an interactive site, a website gives you a home base on the global stage. Find a versatile web company with marketing savvy that offers the best and most innovative services to integrate your web and social media presence.

Resources

> *The Creative Person's Website Builder* by Alannah Moore (hard copy)
>
> *The Creative Person's Website Builder* by Alannah Moore

Audience (Chart 28)

One of the first steps in marketing is answering the question, "Who is going to buy my product or need my services?" Use the Audience Chart to ask that question, and then brainstorm to get more specific answers about your audience.

It's a good idea to write up profiles, imaginary best buyers of your work, so you are clear in your mind who you want as your customers and who can use your product. Then, when you create advertising or social media posts, you'll know how to communicate with and target them through your images and words.

As you grow your business, you will organically get to know your audience. It's necessary to remember your customers at all times while creating a plan, implementing it, and providing your unique product or service. The more clarity you have about your audience, the easier it will be to target your market and spend your marketing time and dollars wisely.

As I. M. Pei, master architect known for his glass pyramid design of the Louvre, said, "Great artists need great clients."

Writer's Platform

In today's marketing world, especially of nonfiction books, it is expected that you will have an author platform and that you will have already made a name for yourself on or off the web before you approach an agent or a publisher. You must create a website with links to Facebook, Instagram, Twitter, and YouTube, and amass "likes" and "followers."

Jane Friedman, writer, blogger, and professor, explains it this way: You have "an ability to sell books because of who you are or who you can reach" (*www.janefriedman.com*). She goes on to say, "Then, as now, publishers and agents seek writers with credentials and authority, who are visible to their target audience as an expert, thought leader, or professional."

The following books can help you build your audience and platform. Again, it's a process. It will take time and energy, but you will be rewarded with an agent and book contract. Think of all the wonderful people you're going to meet globally!

Platform: Get Noticed in a Noisy World by Michael Hyatt

Create Your Writer Platform: The Key to Building an Audience, Selling More Books, and Finding Success as an Author by Chuck Sambuchino

Build Your Author Platform with a Purpose: Marketing Strategies for Writers by Mimika Cooney

Target Location (Chart 29)

Location, location, location!

I love the documentary *Searching for Sugar Man*, the fairy-tale story of talented protest singer/songwriter Sixto Rodriguez, who, when his Motown records flopped in the U.S. in the early 1970s, quit the music scene and became a family man, supporting himself in the construction trade. But unbeknownst to him, in South Africa his two records and songs grew in influence and popularity, and rivaled those of Elvis and the Rolling Stones.

Forty years later, a Swedish filmmaker, Malik Bendjelloul, traveled through Africa searching for a compelling story. He heard of and became intrigued by Rodriguez's music. Bendjelloul looked for and found him in Detroit, living a simple, reclusive life. When Rodriguez was later talked into going to South Africa to perform, he was amazed to find himself playing to huge audiences who loved and adored him. His music even helped sustain the South African movement to end apartheid. See "A Real-Life Fairy Tale, Long in the Making and Set to Old Tunes" by Larry Rohter (July 20, 2012; *www.nytimes.com*).

Remember, if your work isn't received well in one town or city, you must not be discouraged. Learn from the rejection, but keep looking for the right and perfect place for your work. Use this Target Location Chart (29) to give you a broad idea of where your work will be received and go for it.

Sales Venue (Chart 30)

The Sales Venue Chart was created to answer the questions, "Where will my product sell? What venue would be best for me?" The following possible places to market are found on Chart 30. You will want to add your own.

- Art Show
- Church or Spiritual Center
- Coffee House
- College
- Dentist's Office
- First Friday Art Walk
- Gallery
- Healing Arts Office
- Magazine
- Medical Office
- Online Marketplace
- Open Studios
- Other
- Pop Up
- Public Space
- Radio and TV
- Restaurant
- Store
- Street Fair
- Studio
- Website

Online Sales

During this extraordinary time of the COVID-19 pandemic, we have been encouraged to stay home and not venture out much of the time. Yes, it's having a huge impact on retail sales. CNBC News reports, "E-commerce spending in the U.S. is up more than 30 percent . . ." and "there was a whopping 777 percent increase in book purchases. According to the Mastercard Economics Institute, "Consumers across the globe spent $900 billion more at online retailers in 2020 versus the prior two-year trend" (*www.cnbc.com*). For all of us—writers, artists, musicians, and creatives—it's time we increase our web and social media presence and our online sales channels.

Online marketplaces:

○ Musicians can sell their music on their own websites or on other music platforms such as *Bandcamp.com*. (From this website: "Fans have paid artists $578 million using Bandcamp, and $16.9 million in the last 30 days alone.") Or on music download sites such as iTunes, Google Play, or Amazon. See "A Complete Guide to Selling Your Music Online" (*bandzoogle.com*).

○ Writers can sell their books on their own websites or at Amazon. But a popular website that sells books and supports your local indie bookstores is *Bookshop.org*. From their website: "$16,532,302 was raised for local bookstores" as of October 23, 2021.

○ Visual artists have a wealth of online galleries and platforms, such as Saatchi Art, Shopify, Artnet, Artsy, and Etsy.

○ For more ideas about how to sell your products online, see *Sell Online Like a Creative Genius: A Guide for Artists, Entrepreneurs, Inventors, and Kindred Spirits* by Brainard Carey

Social Media Chart (31)

In today's global marketplace, having a social media platform is mandatory if we are to build our audience, reach new customers, and be seen as viable to land those contracts from publishers and galleries. Facebook, Instagram, Twitter, and YouTube are the primary sites for creating a place in the global marketplace, with billions of users both in the United States and worldwide.

The following information was compiled from the article "126 Amazing Social Media Statistics and Facts" on the website Brandwatch, December 30, 2019. (For context, the total worldwide population is 7.8 billion.)

- The Internet has 4.54 billion users.
- There are 3.725 billion active social media users.
- On average, people have 7.6 social media accounts.
- The average time spent on social media is 142 minutes a day.
- Google is the largest search engine with 97 percent of all traffic and billions of searches each day.

The good news: Musicians, artists, and writers can become members of Facebook, Instagram, Twitter, YouTube, and other sites for free. Later, you can choose to advertise for a fee.

Luckily, creatives like making content, and social media gives us a platform to show off our latest work. Here are some of the benefits of creating content and utilizing the tools of social media:

- Helps establish your brand, products, and services.
- Communicates details of events, workshops, new products, and services.
- Helps you stay in touch with customers.
- Enables you to create cost-effective ads, especially when compared to traditional advertising.
- Enables you to track and reach audiences in ads.

- Enables you to advertise to a targeted, large, online audience.
- Improves your search engine visibility.

And the many challenges:

- Using social media can be overwhelming at first, with so much to absorb and learn.
- There's lots of competition.
- Turning followers into customers is challenging.
- Creating posts and original content is time consuming.
- To be effective, you must stay engaged and add content on a regular basis.

Check the Social Media Chart (31) to see where you should start or put your focus with your social media to meet new potential customers.

- **Facebook**—This is the largest social network in the world with a broad audience of both men and women of all ages.
- **Instagram**—Compared to Facebook, Instagram has a younger audience, under thirty, and is especially good for visual artists such as painters and photographers.
- **LinkedIn**—This site focuses on business contacts, networking, and job searching.
- **Other**—Keep your eye out for new, upcoming platforms. It can be advantageous to be an early adopter.
- **Pinterest**—People can find inspiration and ideas for their pastimes and hobbies on this site.
- **Reddit**—This is an American social news aggregation, web content rating, and discussion website.
- **Twitter**—This is the third largest social media platform for mini-posts and sharing links.
- **YouTube**—This online video sharing program is owned by Google. You can create your own programs and have a channel. It is the second-most-visited website in the world.

I have just briefly touched on this immense topic. Please see the websites of each platform. Here are the books that helped me put my toe in the vast pond:

Social Media Marketing by Robert Miller

Avoid Social Media Time Suck by Frances Caballo

Social Media Just for Writers by Frances Caballo

Experiential Exercises

Dowsing

MARKETING (CHART 27)

- Where and how do I begin marketing my art?
- What are the three most important things for me to do?
- What else do I need to focus on?

AUDIENCE (CHART 28)

- Who can I best serve?
- Who else?
- Who needs my services, products, art, music, etc.?

TARGET LOCATION (CHART 29)

- Where will I find my best customers?
- In what location will I find them?
- Where should I market my art?
- Where should I find an agent?
- Is there any place else I can look?

SALES VENUE (CHART 30)

- Where will my product sell?
- What venue would be best for me?
- What else would work for me?

SOCIAL MEDIA CHART (31)

- On what platform should I initially focus my energies?
- What other platform would complement and grow my audience?
- Is there another platform that I will eventually need to expand into?

Journaling

- After reading and dowsing the charts for solutions, what type of marketing appeals to you?
- What types of "friends" would you like to meet? Why or why not?
- What do you have resistance to doing? Why or why not?
- How can you overcome your resistance?
- What excites you about marketing your product or service?

Art

See Chapter 15, "Paint on Your Hands."

CHAPTER 12

Action and Success

Why Not? Isn't It Time?
(Charts 32–33)

Action is the antidote to despair.

—JOAN BAEZ, American folk singer

When you know what you want, it's much easier to clarify your goals, take action, and achieve success. If you're American like me, you most probably have equated success with money, power, and prestige. But on the way to the bank, you might have realized that you also wanted to have a sweet, inspired lifestyle, special time for friends and family, and a life in a holy, blessed place.

Only you can decide what you truly want in your life. It's very much worth the time to take a personal inventory. What do you truly value and love? What are you attracted to in life? What would you like to learn and become skilled at? Where do you want to put your energy? What makes your heart sing? (See the sidebar "Questions to Ponder—Finding Your Personal and Business Vision").

If you're like me, competing parts of yourself may be aspiring to different goals. For instance, I wanted to be both a businesswoman and a mother, and I was never so ambitious as when I was pregnant. The creative energy was flowing while I was working on projects at Apple Computer way back then. I had all these huge ideas pouring through me. I was learning about business and marketing, while taking classes on how to use the Macintosh. I was sad I couldn't complete my Excel class because it was obvious that I was going to be giving birth to my first baby, Adam, any day. Yes, learning about spreadsheets changed my life; for a moment I felt in control of projects and money. But, of course, after the birth of Adam, I lost interest in spreadsheets and fell in love with my precious child.

Again, it happened when I was pregnant with my second baby, Danielle. I felt so powerful and full of the Creative Spirit. When you think about what pregnancy is, you realize the Great Creator Herself is working in and through you to give birth to a new physical being. But after the births of my children, I did have to prioritize my home life and balance it with my business life. In the end, it all worked out because I had lots of help.

In this new world, with so many possibilities, you must go deep within and decide what you truly want. Some dreams are from childhood and adolescence, and some dreams you may discover along the way. I never thought I'd be a painter! I didn't take an art class until I was in my fifties.

If you know what you want, you can make plans for yourself to realize your dreams. If you don't have goals and a plan, most probably your dreams will not come true. It's as simple as that—the bottom line of life. If you don't take time to figure out exactly what you want, you will never arrive. It's like going to an airport to buy a ticket but not knowing which flight to take. The attendant at the ticket counter will not be able to sell you a ticket to the right and perfect place. Yes, you can mosey along, waiting for something to happen to you, but you might wake up realizing you are older, unfulfilled, with a bag of regrets.

After you clarify what you truly want, after you write your plan and begin taking action, you will receive unseen help along the way. Your Creator wants to encourage and support you to fulfill your dreams.

Questions to Ponder—Finding Your Personal and Business Vision

Pick and choose which questions resonate with you and answer to help find your personal and business vision.

○   What do you value and love?

○   What do you wish for?

○   What is your dream?

○   Do you have a mission? Have you been called?

○   How much time would you like for each arena of your life— work, family, and pleasure?

○   If you had full control of your time and structure of your life, what would each day look like?

○   While achieving your goals, what mindset or attitudes would you like to have?

○   What feelings do you want to have while achieving your aspirations?

○   Where would you like to live? And what would your living space look like?

○   Where could you live that would support your creative work and your personal life?

○   What would your workspace look like?

○   How can you do less and earn more?

○   How can you have less work and more time?

○   What can you release from your life and still have a fabulous life?

○   What responsibilities that impede your creative flow can you turn over to others?

○   What would you like to have help with? Who could you have on your team?

○   What are you willing to give up so that you have more time and energy for your work?

○   How many projects would you like to have in a given year?

○   How many events?

○   How much money would you like to make?

- o What kinds of money streams can you envision?
- o Can you think bigger? Can you imagine receiving more time, money, accolades?
- o How can you start moving toward your dreams one day at a time?
- o What will you be giving to others by achieving your goals?
- o What five actions could you take right now, today, that will lead to your success?

Intuitive Action Plan (Chart 32)

I created the Intuitive Action Plan Chart and Form approximately eighteen years ago, and I've used it for coaching my clients to achieve their goals and implement their plans, events, and projects and for developing their businesses. This chart will help you pinpoint next steps, and the powerful one-page form is easy to complete and implement. After completing your Intuitive Action Plan, keep it in a place you see often and refer back to it to monitor your progress. I like checking off my action items.

Seven key steps are found on the Intuitive Action Plan Chart (32) and Form.

Vision "Visioning is a process for creating the life you want. It is a method for finding the dream that lives in your heart and translating it into the world of three dimensions," says Lucia Capacchione in her book, *Visioning*. In your mind, contemplate the vision of what you'd like to achieve and visualize the end product. This can come to you quickly or may take some time. Keep asking to see and hear the words until it is clear in your mind specifically what you want to accomplish and how it actually will manifest. Then write down your vision. Also, see *The Creative Entrepreneur* by Lisa Sonora Beam to visually create your ideas.

Intention Intention can be very potent. Set your true purpose for your project. You can begin by finishing this prompt: "I intend to . . . "

Set Goals Jack Boland, a Unity minister, first taught me about goal setting years ago. He said, "Setting specific, positive, attainable goals—IN WRITING—is the first step in achieving them." Be specific, set a date for accomplishment, review goals often, and celebrate when you reach them. People who set goals and then achieve them produce much more in work and life! Brainstorm what goals you would like to achieve.

Plan for Overcoming Obstacles If you face possible obstacles before they happen, you can ensure that when you encounter them, you already have a plan to overcome them and fulfill your aspirations. Think about anything that might stop you from implementing your plan. It could be a false belief, such as "I'm not smart enough," or a lack of time, money, and/or resources. By having a Plan B (and sometimes Plan C) to overcome the difficulties, you have outwitted your obstacles before they become an issue. Start with naming three obstacles and then brainstorm solutions for each one.

Solutions to Obstacles Brainstorm all your solutions before you need them.

New Belief/Affirmation Clear away old beliefs, such as "Who, me? I'm not creative. I couldn't possibly write a book, give a speech, make a video, *ad infinitum*." Then write a positive statement with your own name in the present tense that affirms that indeed you, and only you, can complete your unique and wonderful project.

Action Items with Completion Dates List five tasks with completion dates. They can be five tasks you could finish in a given morning or bigger tasks for a week, month, or year. You can divide them into short- and long-term action items, and, when necessary, update your plan. Give yourself a reasonable period of time to complete the tasks so you can stay motivated. Play with this list, but make it work for you.

Make a Commitment I always think of W. N. Murray, the Scottish Himalayan expedition leader and author, who said:

> *Until one is committed, there is hesitancy, the chance to draw back, always ineffectiveness. Concerning all acts of initiative (and creation), there is one elementary truth, the ignorance of which kills countless ideas and splendid plans. That the moment one definitely commits oneself, then providence moves, too.*

By making a commitment to Spirit and yourself, you are declaring to the universe that you will complete whatever you set out to do and the universe will come to your personal assistance. See your vision as blessing everyone involved and dedicate your work to the good of all.

You can also take the elements of this plan and turn it into a flowchart or graphic vision board. Doing this will open your mind to other ideas and creativity. You don't have to be pregnant to be filled with the Creative Spirit.

❖ ❖ ❖

With the information you have gathered from these steps, fill out the following Intuitive Action Plan form. You have my permission to copy and use this form in a variety of situations—daily, weekly, monthly, or yearly for planning or for art shows, openings, events, conferences, performances, and product or service rollouts. (See the sample chart.)

Another ploy, borrowed from SARK, inspirational author, is to use energizing and juicy words while creating your plan, such as *brilliant, astounding, incredible, miraculous,* and *stupendous.* I use this trick when I'm stuck, unmotivated, and don't know what to do. Sometimes I make the action items very small. Just by writing out five small actions—*leap* out of bed, *dive* into the computer, *revive* the *wonderful* Word document, review *astounding* copy, and write one first *brilliant* word—I will get back on my slow-moving pony, and eventually she'll gain speed and gallop.

Or I organize *powerful* paints, rearrange *mind-boggling* brushes, find *cool* canvas to paint, *express, amaze,* choose an *inventive* color palette, and *dab* one drop of paint on canvas, and low and behold, I'm laughing at myself and painting.

Or when I'm scared in the middle of the night before a big event or conference, I rewrite the plan before going to sleep or, if awakened, to help me get back to dreamland. I give it to Spirit and ask that She and all the angels, Muses, and forces for good and great be there tomorrow with me! Of course, they will!

I believe in the power of writing an Intuitive Action Plan because writing it out brings it from the mind into physical form.

The Intuitive Action Plan

VISION

_____

_____

INTENTION

_____

_____

GOALS

_____

_____

_____

OBSTACLES   SOLUTIONS

_____   _____

_____   _____

_____   _____

NEW BELIEF/AFFIRMATION

_____

_____

ACTION ITEMS   DATE

_____   _____

_____   _____

_____   _____

_____   _____

COMMITMENT

_____

_____

_____

The Intuitive Action Plan (Sample)

VISION

Joyful, fabulous book with a colorful cover, sixteen intriguing chapters, exciting dowsing, art, and journaling prompts, and thirty-three insightful, Intuitive Creativity Charts.

INTENTION

Have fun, be inspired by Spirit and other creatives, offer all that I have learned over the years, and present the materials in a helpful, friendly, and profound manner to other like-minded spiritual, creative seekers.

GOALS

Write every day, give the book my best hours, and hold the sacred space for this book to come forth. Stay open to guidance from Spirit and the Great Creator.

Complete the book on time and on schedule.

Revise and reinvent social media presence.

OBSTACLES	SOLUTIONS
Negative Thinking	*Clear mind, read positive books daily, meditate*
Distractions	*Notice them, put a time limit on news, refocus*
Tragedy	*Prayer and candles, donations, and be present with friends, family, and clients*

NEW BELIEF/AFFIRMATION

With Spirit, all things are possible. I am a loving, creative writer and person, and the book shines!

ACTION ITEMS	DATE
Reading/Research for Book	*Daily*
Write, write, write	*Daily*
Complete Red Wheel/Weiser Marketing Package	*October 11, 2020*
Edit, revise, and get feedback	*November 15, 2020*
Deliver the manuscript	*December 31, 2020*

COMMITMENT

I, Joan Rose Staffen, commit to brilliantly cocreating The Creative Pendulum *with the angels of light and love and the Great Creator. I align with my High Self and muses. I let go and let Spirit work in and through me. All, all is in divine order.*

I realize this is a short section for a major undertaking! Please see my book *Divination & Action* for other ideas and a complete set of Intuitive Business Charts.

Success (Chart 33)

Success is an American word, an idea, a brass ring. If we're in business, we're always attempting to achieve material wealth, sometimes at any cost—sacrificing family and friends and a balanced life. Traditionally, in American culture, success in the arts has meant wealth and fame consigned to mass media popular writers, painters, film stars, singers, musicians, and performing artists.

Have you ever seen Tony Robbins at a success seminar? I have. He was very entertaining and motivating; he got the audience revved up, and soon we were all screaming. At expensive seminars, he helps you find a bigger self who can also fire walk. Many have followed in his footsteps! But some can't copy his strenuous, outsized style. I am a creative spiritual seeker, looking for a quieter, more satisfying lifestyle that suits me, meanwhile making authentic connections with others along the way and, of course, having time for my creations.

In contrast to Robbins's style is that of a deep, popular thinker from the nineteenth century, Ralph Waldo Emerson, who was at that time, America's most widely known and popular essayist, lecturer, philosopher, and poet. He defined success this way:

To laugh often and much;
to win the respect of intelligent people
and the affection of children;
to earn the appreciation of honest critics

and endure the betrayal of false friends;
to appreciate beauty,
to find the best in others,
to leave the world a little better;
whether by a healthy child,
a garden patch or a redeemed social condition;
to know even one life has breathed
easier because you have lived.
This is the meaning of success.

I have always loved Emerson's definition, which is so grounded in being a whole human being first.

While writing this section, I thought about not only my successes but naturally also my failures. Yes, I have had my share—in relationships and in business. I have had economic roadblocks (recessions), devastating life events (death), and have even lived through natural disasters (earthquakes and fires). Life has not always been easy. I haven't always been successful and accomplished what I wanted in the moment. I've had times I had to let go of my immediate desires, dreams, and plans just to survive until there was a later time when I could thrive. I had to ask for spiritual guidance, courage to just keep showing up, doing the next right thing, praying much, and surrendering to a higher plan.

What life lessons did I learn? Persistence, humility, patience, forgiveness of myself and others. Ann Patchett, my favorite author, says, "Forgiveness. The ability to forgive oneself. Stop here for a few breaths and think about this because it is the key to making art, and very possibly the key to finding any semblance of happiness in life" (*www.brainpickings.org*).

As we open to the Creative Spirit, show up daily to do our best, and do the next right thing—moving the right foot, the left foot—we are on the path and achieving results. Yes, I put fame, financial success, and wealth on this chart, as material success will come to some of us, but for many, it is the inner, intrinsic rewards that will bless our lives.

So, how do you measure success for yourself? This chart will help you define your own version of success and help you reach for your own dreams.

Letting Go of Fear and Finding Success Worksheet

Take a few moments to answer the following questions. Do the exercise rapidly so you can write and not edit or criticize yourself as you write.

- Are you stopping yourself from becoming all you could become? You can use your pendulum and dowse the *yes/no* answer.
- Who would you be if you were fully successful? Dream big and be as wild as you can to answer this question. What do you have to lose? Also see the Success Chart (33).
- What would achievement look like in your world?
- What is your specific fear?
- Would you have to leave anyone behind if you were successful?
- Would someone be upset or angry at you for being successful?
- Whose self-image would you have to let go of if you were successful?
- What else would you have to give up?
- Are you angry you're not more successful financially? Why?
- What does success look like to you now? Would you like to dream even bigger?

On the Success Chart (33), I list nineteen rewards of success. Based on who you are and what you truly value, dowse with your pendulum to discover what you truly want.

- Appreciation
- Created
- Fame
- Fortune
- Friends
- Personal Growth
- Learned

- Loved
- Met Your Goals
- New Mindset
- Other
- Overcame Fear
- Persisted
- Respect

- Self-Supporting
- Showed Up
- Wealth
- Your Own Boss
- Your Own Style

Success Comes in Many Sizes

Acknowledging the success that we've achieved is very important. I asked my fellow artists, "What has been your happiest, most
beloved, amazing accomplishment?"

Being mindful and awake!

—MARIA CHOMENTOWSKI, visual artist

Dry and Humid Patterns, an installation. I realized my skills
grew, and I pushed myself in new ways. The installation was
the biggest, most in-depth piece I have created. I love multiples and the idea of filling up space with art.

—MAHA TAITANO, sculptor and installation artist

Establishing a successful band and being a respected leader
in my artistic community.

—SANDRA SHAMMA, singer and songwriter

I have warm memories of my BFA exhibition, Antithesis,
from 2017 at San Jose State University, where I hung my
paintings in the largest studio space on campus and invited
friends and family to the reception. My mom got me a delicious chocolate cake from the Buttery Bakery, and Alfredo
brought me tulips. I spent a year making those paintings.

—DANI TORVIK, visual artist

When my partner, Deanie, and I lived in Mexico, a gallery
asked me to create a series of three sculptures. I had all the
tools I needed, a time frame for completion, and three huge
stones on my table on a concrete slab next to our cabin
between the sea and the mountains. I thank my Mexican
compadres whose land and stone it was.

—HAPPI CAMPBELL, sculptor and painter

My business being a success after seven years!

—SONIA LE, fashion designer

Finishing my novels.

—ELIZABETH MCKENZIE, novelist

Keeping an active art practice for fifty years and counting.

—MARGARET NIVEN, visual artist and college teacher

Instead of a specific moment, it's more about a feeling I get when a client expresses how much my services have made them happy. Those moments are my greatest joy.

—KRISTA POLLOCK, chef/baker

Seeing my first book, *Earth, My Witness*, in print!

—MAGDALENA MONTAGNE, poet and poetry teacher

Founding the *Catamaran Literary Reader*.

—CATHERINE SEGURSON, founder of the *Catamaran Literary Reader*

Experiential Exercises

Dowsing

INTUITIVE ACTION PLAN CHART (32)

- What is working?
- What do I need to focus on?
- What am I achieving right now?
- Where would I like to be in three months, six months, a year?

SUCCESS CHART (33)

- What do I want for myself, my life, my art career?
- What is my deepest desire for success?
- What other benefit of success would I enjoy?

Journaling

Write your Intuitive Action Plan now!

CHAPTER 13

Coach Yourself to Personal Success

Success is not final; failure is not fatal:
It is the courage to continue that counts.

—WINSTON S. CHURCHILL

Now that you've learned how to use the pendulum and been introduced to the Intuitive Creativity Charts, it's time to jump into the juicy stuff. Haven't you always wanted to be able to ask and receive answers from your inner High Self and your Guides? Haven't you wanted a personal map so you knew the way forward and the route to take?

As you start practicing a few times a week or daily using the charts, you will notice that you are learning and integrating your knowledge on multiple levels. It's as if your intuitive, psychic mind is awakening and developing. In Elizabeth Brown's book, *Dowsing: The Ultimate Guide for the 21st Century*, she cites experiments that demonstrated when gifted dowsers are tested, their minds are operating on many levels at once—alpha, beta, delta, and theta! That's why you may feel more balanced after a dowsing session.

In my introductory pendulum classes, after practicing for just a few minutes to use the charts, most people are able to take the leap and give each other insights and mini-readings for themselves. As a teacher, I find this moment most satisfying. As I see people pairing off and reading for each other, I sit back and watch them—amazed at everyone's innate, intuitive abilities and how people love helping each other.

My students are exploring a new, revolutionary divination system (based on ancient wisdom). While one person holds the Personal Inventory Form, asks questions, and fills out the document, the other divines with the pendulum and charts. I hear laughter and surprise. At the end of the session, people—who just an hour before did not know each other—now hug and thank one another.

This is evidence that the answers are already inside of us, and through the use of the pendulum and charts, words act as the small and large clues to life and creativity. The key words found on the charts help unlock our subconscious and super-consciousness. Suddenly, we are able to access the inner intuitive world. Through using the pendulum with the Intuitive Creativity Charts, you receive inner knowledge and specific answers.

If you haven't already, review each chart—asking questions and receiving answers. The more familiar you are with the charts, the easier it will be to coach yourself and to go from chart to chart. Again, the more specific your questions, the clearer your answers. And just to confuse and amuse us—sometimes the answers are literal, and sometimes they are more metaphorical in nature.

Spiritually Prepare to Give Yourself Readings

Sometimes you will be more centered than other times, but it's important to always take a few minutes to prepare for a reading for yourself or others. After all, it is our connection to Spirit and our High Self that makes our readings so powerful.

Here are the steps to guide you.

Time

Give yourself the gift of time—fifteen minutes, thirty is better! This is your time with Spirit.

Create a Sacred Space

Have a comfortable, beautiful, private space to do your readings. You may want to create an altar with your favorite crystals, fresh flowers, candles, and other items of spiritual and creative significance to you. Your space should be clean and without clutter. Don't forget to empty the trash too. After all, the angels and spirit guides are attending your important meeting. Then clear your space with your pendulum, and if you feel the need, double-check that you are clear and all is clear with the Clearing Needed Chart (3). Then, light a candle to create sacred space, and say a prayer or affirmation requesting assistance from your Spirit helpers, asking that the reading be from the highest levels and that it be for the highest good for all.

Center and Breathe

Take a deep centering breath and do a short centering meditation to quiet the mind and connect with your creative source. (See Chapter 2 for ideas and a centering meditation.) Sometimes I listen to peaceful music beforehand to help me enter the blessed space for readings. Incorporate your own spiritual tools that connect you to Source.

After you've been doing this for a while, you will more naturally go into dowsing and divining mode, and you will know you are there. But it helps to check off this list in your mind and to ask your pendulum if you are grounded, centered, and ready to begin.

Ask, Using Your Pendulum

- Am I working with my High Self?
- Am I in a centered, neutral place?
- Will my answers be correct?
- Do I have permission to do this reading and to work on this person(s)?

Write Down Your Answers

Keeping track of the pendulum work you are doing in your readings is very rewarding and fun. You will be amazed. Use the Intuitive Creativity Coaching Worksheets found later in this chapter. Please feel free to copy these forms.

Thank your spirit guides for their help!

You are willing, curious, and I am sure you have many questions. I found this to be such an exciting time in my learning process. I learned I could ask the pendulum anything! I had only one or two charts at the time, but it seemed to work. In the coaching system, you will have thirty-three charts to explore with your pendulum, your new friend.

Before taking any action with the insights you receive for the larger questions, check out your intuition with a friend, partner, or mentor. Use both your rational and intuitive mind to clarify decisions.

Use the Short Free Form Method or the more complete Intuitive Creativity Coaching Worksheets found in this chapter to assess where you are and where you want to go.

Short Free Form Creativity Coaching Session

Sometimes, we just need a quick check-in with ourselves, and we can go directly to the chart we need. Perhaps we have only a few minutes, but we want to check our intuition. You can start at the Table of Charts and just ask, "What do I need?" Or you can go directly to the chart your intuition is telling you to go to and ask, "What do I need?"

How to Use the Intuitive Creativity Coaching Worksheets

I created the following worksheets found in this chapter to guide your Intuitive Creativity Coaching for yourself. (Feel free to copy and use.) Also, you will be directed by your own intuition to ask further questions. Later, you will find you know the process so well that you will no longer need to consult the worksheet, but it's great to have a template as you learn.

1. **State the Issue(s).** Clarify the issue. You can write it in question form.

2. **Research.** You are using the pendulum and charts to ask questions and find answers. You can begin by asking general questions, but the more specific your questions, the better your answers will be. You will grow in this questioning skill as you gain experience.

3. **Find Solutions.** What would help in this particular situation? [Table of Charts, Solutions Chart (10), Artist Needs Chart (11), or some other chart.]

4. **Clear the Issue and the Client.**

5. **Take Action.** Help the client find three to five actions with dates to complete to move their creativity forward.

6. **Write an Affirmation.** This affirmation will support the client through their process. Remember to put it into the present tense using their name.

7. **Say Thank You to the Creative Spirit and Your Guides.**

After finishing these worksheets, you will have a complete assessment of your creative life. You'll be amazed at your own progress. You have come so far!

But if this system feels confusing, be patient with yourself. You are learning how to use it on many levels of your mind. Everything important takes time to learn. If you get frustrated, rest for a while; put your pendulum down, make a cup of coffee or tea, and come back to it later.

It's also fun to teach a friend as you learn to use the pendulum and charts, and then you can coach each other. In time, when you feel comfortable with your pendulum and the Intuitive Creativity Chart, you can give Intuitive Creativity Coaching Sessions to family and friends. In the next chapter, we'll continue the adventure.

#1 Personal Assessment
(Intuitive Creativity Coaching Worksheet)

Date _____

1. State the Issue(s).

What is the primary issue(s)?

_____

_____

2. Research (Sample Questions).

Is clearing needed? See Yes/No Clearing Chart (1).

What needs clearing? See Clearing Needed Chart (3). Then be sure to clear the energy with the clearing signal. See Yes/No Clearing Chart (1).

_____

_____

What is needed? See Table of Charts or Artist Needs Chart (11).

_____

_____

Inspiration? See Inspiration Chart (6).

_____

_____

Are there any negative beliefs? See Negative Beliefs Chart (7).

_____

_____

_____

Are there any distractions? See Distractions Chart (8).

_____

_____

Is there anything blocking creativity? Use Creative Blocks
Chart (9).

_____

_____

3. Find Solutions.

What solutions would help? See Solutions Chart (10).

What else would help right now? (See Table of Charts.)

_____

_____

4. Take Action. What can I do to move forward? (Brainstorm
your answers.)

Action   Completion Date

_____   _____

_____   _____

_____   _____

_____   _____

5. Clear Yourself and the Issue.

_____

_____

6. Write an Affirmation for Yourself.

_____

_____

7. Say Thank You to the Creative Spirit and Your Guides!

#2 Personal Assessment
(Intuitive Creativity Coaching Worksheet)

Date _____

1. State the Issue(s).

What is the primary issue(s)?

_____

_____

2. Research.

Who am I? What creative ventures do I want to pursue? What is my creative identity? See Creative Identity Chart (15) and Charts 16–20.

_____

_____

Where am I in my creative process? See Creative Process Chart (21).

_____

_____

3. Find Solutions.

Where should I focus my energies? See Table of Charts and Creative Process Chart (21).

_____

_____

What do I need to focus on in my business? What else? See Business of Art Chart (25).

_____

_____

_____

What income streams should I pursue? How can I increase my business? What would I like to try next? See Income Streams Chart (26).

_____

_____

_____

What aspects of marketing should I explore? See Marketing Chart (27).

_____

_____

_____

Who is my audience? See Audience Chart (28).

_____

_____

_____

What location should I target? See Target Location Chart (29).

_____

_____

_____

In what venue would my work sell? See Sales Venue Chart (30).

_____

_____

_____

Where online could I improve my presence? Which social media platform should I focus on? Any other? See Social Media Chart (31).

_____

_____

_____

Should I create an Intuitive Action Plan? (Yes/No) What area should I focus on? See Intuitive Action Plan Chart (32) and Intuitive Action Plan Worksheet (Chapter 12).

_____

_____

_____

_____

What aspects of success do I hope to gain by my intentions, goals, and actions? See Success Chart (33).

_____

_____

_____

_____

4. Take Action.

What three to five tasks can I do or take?

Action   Completion Date

_____   _____

_____   _____

_____   _____

_____   _____

_____   _____

5. Clear Yourself and the Issue.

6. Write an Affirmation.

_____

_____

_____

_____

7. Say Thank You to the Creative Spirit and Your Guides!

Experiential Exercises

Dowsing Prompt

Practice coaching yourself!

Journaling

- Are you more in touch with your inner self and your outer actions using this process? Why or why not?
- What is working for you while dowsing and coaching yourself? What do you want to improve on?
- What kind of growth can you see as you are coaching yourself with this new process?
- What are your best "aha" moments while coaching yourself?

Art

See Chapter 15, "Paint on Your Hands."

CHAPTER 14

Coach Others

Discover Their Gifts and Motivate Them to Take Action

*Creativity is not a talent or ability. It is the fruit
of a person's decision to matter.*

—ERIC MAISEL, *Become a Creativity Coach Now!*

After twenty years of giving readings and coaching sessions, I still love the magic and transformation that happens when I work one-on-one with clients. It's as if we enter a sacred space, and in one short hour, my client and I have discussed, explored, and identified many problems, researched the issues, found solutions, and cleared the rubble of the past and present. Then, we put together a mini-action plan, and clients leave knowing the bigger picture and the next steps in their creative journey.

The Intuitive Creativity Coaching system taught in this book differs from other coaching methods in that the coach not only relies on analytical skills but also offers the powerful addition of intuition—that human power to access one's own truth.

You too can learn how to be an Intuitive Creativity Coach for others. This will take much practice and time, but through using the

Intuitive Creativity Coaching system and other methods, you will achieve great satisfaction. You will help others find their talents and abilities, and give them the gift of courage and the will to take action.

Most creativity coaches have a background in the arts, and they come into coaching having gained practical life, work, and creative experience. Now, with your own hard-earned wisdom and talents, you can help others. Remind yourself of all you've done in life, business, and the creative realms. What are the gifts you have to share?

Coaching simply is the practice of helping others achieve their hopes and dreams. When we were children and teenagers, most of us had coaches in sports—men and women who taught us the skills, discipline, and team spirit to mold us into better people and excellent baseball, football, soccer players, or swimmers (like myself). Today, the coaching model has been borrowed and expanded to include life and business, and creativity coaches, who mentor and challenge people to be their best selves, initiate and complete projects, and press forward with their dreams.

When offering Intuitive Creativity Coaching to others, remember your purpose is to support the person and their vision. With the light of higher forces, help your clients understand their role, creative work, and any actions they can take to fulfill their mission. Let the coaching session be an optimistic, encouraging time, and let the higher energy forces flow through your words.

You must let go your own opinions, judgments, and ideas as to what is right or wrong for a client. As a coach and facilitator, you are the neutral party to let the Higher Source flow through you, the pendulum, and the Intuitive Creativity Charts. As your dowsing skills and intuitive senses develop, you will be able to recognize when you are being impartial and unbiased.

Coaching can be similar to "talk therapy." When you are a sounding board for others, people uncover their own answers and truths. As a coach, you need to listen intently to what clients are saying. There is a well-used technique that will serve you and your clients well: Repeat back to clients what they have just said to you because this helps verify with them what they meant to say.

Additionally, your role as coach is to ask relevant questions to help uncover underlying issues and subconscious drives. Sometimes, it's

important to stop a client when they have said something significant, and they need to reflect on what they have just declared.

Listening is itself an art form. When you listen intently, your own
mind is quiet, and you absorb on many levels what the client is saying and not saying. Also, you can look at their body language. Ask
yourself what their body language is telling you.

One group that puts listening at the center of its organizational
heart is The Center for Nonviolent Communication; their ideas are
practiced and taught worldwide to help diverse people and groups
communicate. This system is based on the teachings of Gandhi,
who helped free India from British rule and famously said, "Be the
change that you wish to see in the world."

> *With Nonviolent Communication (NVC) we learn to
> hear our own deeper needs and those of others. Through
> its emphasis on deep listening—to ourselves as well as
> others—NVC helps us discover the depth of our own
> compassion. (www.cnvc.org)*

Often, a client's issues are organizational: Creatives get overwhelmed and don't know where to start or what project to focus on.
Should it be the large project that will elevate their creative work,
or should the client focus on the smaller projects that bring in the
money but no longer offer creative satisfaction?

Sometimes, the issue is discovering deep inner negative beliefs,
often from childhood, that unconsciously control their thoughts and
behavior. Negative beliefs can pop up in many forms, be subtle or
not, and literally stop them in their tracks. Dowse with the Negative
Beliefs Chart (7).

Or perhaps the client is distracted or creatively blocked? Dowse
with the Distractions Chart (8) and Creative Blocks Chart (9). Find
answers on the Solutions Chart (10). You can be of assistance to your
clients by pulling the weeds out of the gardens in their minds and
hearts. This is an ongoing process, but it takes just a few minutes.

Often, the work of a coach is to assist clients to make larger decisions, such as which opportunities to say *yes* to and what to say *no*
to. You can listen, reflect back to the client, and use the Time and
Percent Chart (2) to help answer these questions. Ask "What is the

positive?" and "What is the negative?" of the situation. "What will be gained? What doors of opportunity could open?"

Sometimes, I tell a client beforehand that I would like to see a positive outcome for a specific challenge, so I am a little biased. Then, I go into the "neutral" space and ask the question and check the chart. I tell the truth in a loving, compassionate manner, even if the client does not want to hear it. Your words have significance, and people will remember what you tell them, so err on the side of caution. A softer approach gives clients room to make their own choices, and in making their own choices, most clients will follow through with action items that you create together.

In a *Course in Miracles*, we learn that "to teach is to learn, so that the teacher and the learner are the same" (*Course in Miracles*, Teachers' Manual 1–5). When you coach others, you will be learning profound lessons as well. I think that is why I have loved coaching others so much. Not only have I helped another, but I continue growing spiritually and creatively. Sometimes what I say to the client is also what I need to hear myself.

Coaching Guidelines for Each Session

- Before the session, spiritually prepare yourself. (See Chapters 2 and 12.)

- Set a timer for the allotted time, so when you go into the coaching zone, you can relax.

- Begin each session with a short centering prayer such as: I ask in your holy names, for your presence, guidance, clarity, and healing on any and all issues that are revealed today. Help us follow your guidance and take action, knowing that your will for us and love is good, wise, and often fun.

- Explain the pendulum and the Intuitive Creativity Charts and how the system works if a person is not familiar with them. This explanation usually just takes a moment and fascinates some clients.

- Spend a few minutes listening to their creative, life, and business issues that have brought your client to you today.

- Help them clarify their primary issues. Often, this will help make clear their questions and aid in finding true answers.

- Use the Creativity Coaching Forms found at the end of this chapter to guide you.

- As the trust deepens between you as you listen, clients relax and are able to speak more openly.

- Some clients like to meet once a week, once a month, or as they need your help. This meeting can be via phone, Internet, or in person. (During the pandemic, meetings have taken place via phone and Zoom, which seems to work just as well as in person.) Sometimes it's helpful to have an initial in-person meeting to establish trust and connection with a client.

- I like using a clipboard when I give readings so I can easily take notes. Taking notes helps me stay neutral and gives me a place to write observations for myself. For ongoing client meetings, you also can refer back to client notes that you've kept in a folder.

Intuitive Creativity Coaching Worksheets for Clients

The preceding chapter introduced you to the Intuitive Creativity Coaching Worksheets to use for yourself. The following forms are almost identical, but they focused on the client.

When working with new clients, you may need two coaching sessions to cover the Client Assessment Form and the Client Gifts, Identity, Process, and Action Assessment Form. If you use them as an evaluation in the beginning of your relationship with your client and keep records, you can see how well your client is progressing. You can make a copy for your client so they know where they were when they started working with you.

I created the Client Ongoing Coaching for Success Form for continuing work with clients.

You can also use the Intuitive Action Plan found in Chapter 12 to help clients plan for projects, events, launches, overall marketing strategies, and business plans.

You now have many tools to help you begin Intuitive Creativity Coaching. You can copy these three Coaching Forms for your own use. As your own Intuitive Creativity Coaching advances and you become more adept, you will follow your own inner guidance as to what the client needs, and perhaps, create your own forms and processes.

Client Assessment Form—Intuitive Creativity Coaching

Name _____

Date _____

1. Issue. What is the primary issue(s)?

_____

_____

2. Research (Sample Questions).

Is clearing needed? See Yes/No Clearing Chart (1).

What needs clearing? See Clearing Needed Chart (3).

_____

_____

What is needed? See Table of Charts or Artist Needs Chart (10).

_____

_____

Inspiration? See Inspiration Chart (6).

_____

_____

_____

Are there any negative beliefs? See Negative Beliefs Chart (7).

_____

_____

_____

Are there any distractions? See Distractions Chart (8).

_____

_____

_____

Is there anything blocking creativity? See Creative Blocks Chart (9).

_____

_____

3. Find Solutions.

What solutions would help? See Solutions Chart (10).

_____

_____

_____

What else would help right now? (See Table of Charts.)

_____

_____

_____

4. What Tasks Can Be Done? (Brainstorm your answers with the client.)

Action   Completion Date

_____   _____

_____   _____

_____   _____

_____   _____

5. Clear the Client and the Issue(s).

6. Write an Affirmation with the Client.

_____

_____

_____

7. Say a Prayer of Thanks to the Creative Spirit.

Client Gifts, Identity, Process, and Action Assessment Form

Name _____

Date _____

1. Issue(s).

What is the primary issue(s)?

_____

_____

_____

_____

2. Research.

What is the client's creative identity? What creative ventures does the client want to pursue? What are their gifts? See Creative Identity Chart (15) and Charts 15–20.

_____

_____

_____

_____

Where are they in their creative process? See Creative Process Chart (21).

_____

_____

_____

3. Solutions.

Where should they focus their energies? See Creative Process Chart (21).

_____

_____

_____

What do they need to focus on in their business? What else? See Business of Art Chart (25).

_____

_____

_____

What income streams should they pursue? How can they increase their business? What would they like to try next? See Income Streams Chart (26).

_____

_____

_____

What marketing avenues should they explore? See Marketing Chart (27).

_____

_____

_____

Who is their audience? See Audience Chart (28).

_____

_____

What location should they target? See Target Location Chart (29).

_____

_____

In what venue would their work sell? See Sales Venue Chart (30).

_____

_____

Where online do they need to improve their presence? Which social media platform should they focus on? Any other? See Social Media Chart (31).

_____

_____

Should they create an Intuitive Action Plan? (Yes/No) What area should they focus on? See Intuitive Action Plan Chart (32) and Intuitive Action Plan Worksheet.

_____

_____

What aspects of success do they hope to gain by their intentions, goals, and actions? See Success Chart (33).

_____

_____

4. Action.

What three to five things can they can do to move forward?

Action   Completion Date

_____   _____

_____   _____

_____   _____

_____   _____

_____   _____

5. Clear Your Client and the Issue(s).

6. Help the Client Write an Affirmation to Support Their New Mindset and Follow Through on Actions and Plans.

_____

_____

7. Say a Prayer of Thanks to the Creative Spirit.

Client Ongoing Coaching for Success Form

Name _____

Date _____

1. Primary Problems, Issues, and Challenges.

Listen and help the client state them as clearly as possible.

_____

_____

2. Research.

What does the client need? Creatively, emotionally, spiritually, mentally, or physically?

_____

_____

3. Solutions.

What will help the client? How can their needs be fulfilled? What are other solutions?

_____

_____

4. Clearing.

Clear the issues, distractions, blocks, old beliefs and, in general, the client.

5. Action.

What positive actions can they take in what time frame?

Tasks   Completion Date

_____   _____

_____   _____

_____   _____

6. Affirmation.

Help the client write an affirmation to support their new mindset and follow through on actions and plans.

_____

_____

7. Say a Prayer of Thanks to the Creative Spirit.

Completing the Session

At the end of your session with your client, double-check and verify that the person has received what they need during the session. I ask:

- How do you feel?
- Do you have any further questions that you want to discuss?
- Do you need clarity on anything else?

I always thank my client and remind them to take it easy and drink water, as we have done deep clearing and creative work.

After I am off the phone or after a client leaves, I take some deep breaths, wash my hands, and have a glass of water to refresh my own energy. I thank the angels and Spirit for the assistance they gave me in the coaching sessions.

A Few More Tips on Coaching

- Review each of the charts in this book until you are familiar with them. As you use the charts often, your readings and coaching sessions will improve. Soon, you will become more intuitive and psychic.

- As an Intuitive Creativity Coach, you are holding the space and energy for your clients to transform. You are giving them the view from the highest level and then helping them take practical action to move forward to a more positive future.

- You are helping your clients be accountable to start and finish projects. For some, it's easy to begin and hard to complete. Do you know how many unfinished novels are lying in drawers? Or unfinished paintings? Or art in a closet because the artist didn't have a coach to say, "Do it anyway." It's so fabulous to have one special person helping another be their best self.

- Often, on some level, people already know what they need to do. By holding the sacred space for them to tell you their deepest desires, truths, and secrets, you give them the opportunity to reveal these dreams to you and to themselves. Then they will come to the answers themselves and have "aha" moments!

- Hold the revealed information confidential. You will be helping them feel safe and loved.

- Know you do not have all the answers. Sometimes answers— especially to larger issues—hide until the person is ready for them. But it is so great to ask the questions and ponder them over time. Then the answers will be revealed in an opportune manner.

- ***Remember that you are not a doctor or therapist.*** At times people with complex problems will arrive. Lovingly refer them to others with more experience: a doctor, trained therapist, or other professional.

- Get coaching yourself so you continue to understand the intuitive coaching process. This coaching can be with a professional or a friend, but it will keep you on the transformative path.

Please also see my other books that offer Intuitive Coaching Charts for health, life, and business:

The Book of Pendulum Healing: Charting Your Healing Course for Mind, Body, & Spirit
Divination & Joy: Intuitive Tools for an Inspired Life
Divination & Action: Intuitive Tools for an Inspired Work Life

Also see:

Eric Maisel's *Become a Creativity Coach Now!*

Creativity coaching courses that can augment your own creativity and help your future creativity clients are available:

See Eric Maisel's website at *ericmaisel.com*
Creativity Coaching Association at *creativitycoachingassociation.com*.

Experiential Exercises

Dowsing

To become a better Intuitive Creativity Coach, review each of the charts in this book until you are familiar with them. As you use the charts often, your readings and coaching sessions will improve. Soon, you will become more intuitive and psychic.

Practice coaching others and giving them Intuitive Creativity Coaching Sessions.

Journaling

- How have you transformed as you've worked through this book and completed the exercises? Make a list of five to seven breakthroughs.

- How will you stay motivated to use dowsing, the Intuitive Creativity Charts, and the Creativity Coaching method for yourself and others in the future?

- Who else in your life can you teach to dowse and use the methods in this book?

Art

See Chapter 15, "Paint on Your Hands."

CHAPTER 15

Paint on Your Hands

Art Prompts

They taught me what I knew to be true in writing, but now had to learn in another medium: that creativity is a process, that it takes practice, that it is full of surprise and discovery and cannot be known ahead of time.

—NATALIE GOLDBERG, foreword to *Life, Paint and Passion: Reclaiming the Magic of Spontaneous Expression* by Michele Cassou and Stewart Cubley

I was a writer before I was a painter. A profound dream spurred me on to begin painting. I began with little 3" × 5" canvases—it felt safe to start small. I began with Golden acrylics because I saw my girlfriend paint with them and fell in love with the colors.

I have learned in life it's okay not to know everything. In fact, it can be fun and give you an advantage. Perhaps you didn't know you could just paint and not worry about the painting not looking like something. You could just enjoy the colors of the paint and putting them on canvas or paper and seeing what happens. You could play with the colors and different paintbrushes. You don't have to understand color theory.

One of the first things people most often say in my introduction to the Artist's Way class is, "Oh, I can't paint." I always follow that comment by saying, "We start with finger painting." Then we all laugh, because somewhere deep inside of us, there is a child that definitely knows how to finger paint!

Another thing that happened: I started intuitively hearing my paintings talk to me. Don't tell anyone—they'll think I'm crazy—but I felt the energy of the paintings speaking. Paintings told me when to stop, what they needed, their names, and that they were gifts for different people.

A year later, an art teacher told me what I was doing was called "Process Painting" as offered in Michele Cassou's and Stewart Cubley's book, *Life, Paint, and Passion*. I bought the book and felt reassured. I was later introduced to Flora Bowley and her process called "Brave Intuitive Painting," which definitely resonated with me. Both these similar processes give you a unique way to explore painting before you study techniques and color theory.

I created the fun exercises included in this chapter to help beginners spark their own brave, intuitive creative within. We'll make a pendulum, draw simple pictures, create collage, finger paint, pick up paintbrushes, and experience color. It's a process of remembering how to play as we did when we were children, without judgment and without expecting ourselves to know everything. It's about process rather than the final product.

A few notes: We start with acrylic paint rather than oil or watercolors because acrylic can be more forgiving. You can layer your canvas, experiment, paint over what's not working, emphasize other regions of your painting, and even wash your brushes in water. But acrylics will stain your clothes, furniture, and the floor, so use a drop cloth and wear an old T-shirt or an apron. Let yourself get messy if you can. Messy is good.

If you can afford it, buy the best supplies because they do make a difference. For instance, buy professional-grade acrylics rather than studio-grade acrylics, as professional grade acrylics have more pigment and give your paintings a brighter glow.

I call these exercises "prompts" because they are jumping-off points to help you begin making, collaging, and painting. If you find you are going in a different direction than the prompt, just know you're going in the right direction for yourself.

Mindset for All Art Exercises

- Take a few moments to connect with Spirit.
- Breathe in light consciously as you delve into the creative realm.
- Practice open-mindedness and nonjudgment as you let yourself explore.
- Love yourself unconditionally while you create.
- *Just begin and see what happens!*

The short mindset form of this exercise is *connect, breathe, open, and love unconditionally,* which you will be reminded of in each art exercise.

Repeat the following affirmation (or create one of your own) and breathe as you say it:

> *I am beloved by the Great Creator, whose sacred light is also within me. As I play, I express my divine creativity and reveal myself to myself. I am both safe and courageous as I allow myself to explore the unknown. All is well.*

Now, post this affirmation in a place you will see it often, perhaps in your art space that you're now excited to create. Playing music can also be helpful. Experiment with music and see what works for you.

Additionally, I use the term *suggested materials*. Please use what works for you and what your budget can afford. Also, I offer time recommendations, primarily to reassure you that these exercises can be done in a short amount of time.

1. Make or Shop for Your Pendulum

First, connect, breathe, open, and love unconditionally.

Making your own pendulum is pleasurable. You might want to use a pendant and chain from your own jewelry box or find a pointed object that can be hung on a string, such as a crystal, gem, or stone. Attach it to a four- to five-inch or longer string, a silver or gold chain, or silk cord if you prefer. The weight of the pendulum should be in proportion to the weight of the string or chain so that they are in balance with each other. For instance, you would want to use a heavy chain with a larger pendant.

Alternatively, if you already bead or are interested in beading, you can go to a local store and find materials to make a chain with fastenings for the pendulum. The important thing is to remember the pendulum must swing to and fro unencumbered, and you should feel comfortable using it.

If you don't have the materials to make a pendulum, perhaps you'd like to go shopping for one. This can be an exploratory adventure at a crystal store, a New Age bookstore, or online. You will find many different pendulums ranging from inexpensive to very expensive.

For right now, the most important thing is that you like your pendulum and that it feels comfortable in your hand. You may be attracted to crystal pendulums. If so, choose a color that you love. It's important to buy a pendulum with a pointed end so that you can use it with the Intuitive Creativity Charts. Some people like more than one pendulum just for fun. See what calls to you.

2. Organize Your Play Materials

First, connect, breathe, open, and love unconditionally.

Now, it's time to organize your art materials. Check to see if you have any tucked away. This can be fun and inspiring. Aren't your fingers itching to start playing? You can put your supplies in a box or an art storage cabinet. Find a space for your art materials so that when you do your exercises, you can easily pull them out and begin.

Do you have the following?

- Drawing pad
- Postcards, greeting cards, or magazines to recycle and repurpose
- Colored or craft paper
- Acrylic paints
- Watercolors
- Felt-tipped pens
- Colored pencils
- Glue sticks
- Glue
- Scissors
- Watercolor paper, mixed media paper, or canvas

Fill In Your Art Supplies

Now, visit your local art store or go online at *Amazon.com* or *DickBlick* *.com* to purchase the supplies listed here. It's fun to shop intuitively with your pendulum and with your intuitive senses open. Just ask, "What do I need? What do I want?"

I remember the first time I went to our local Palace Art store as an adult. I was nervous and excited. What if someone knew I wasn't a real artist? What if I bought the wrong supplies? What if someone caught me looking at paper? What if?

There is much to choose from online. Here is a list of supplies I found at Amazon:

- AmazonBasics Sketch and Drawing Art Pencil Kit, seventeen-piece set
- Fluid Watercolor Paper 850088 140LB Hot Press 8" × 8" and/or 12" × 12" block
- Golden Fluid Acrylic, one-ounce set of ten assorted colors
- Liquitex Gloss Acrylic Fluid Medium and Varnish, eight ounces
- Conda foam brush set of all sizes
- Yelico Acrylic Paintbrush Set, twenty pieces for acrylic, oil, watercolor and gouache
- Uni-posca paint marker pen, fine point, set of eight (PC-3M8C), multicolor

Now, I hope I haven't overwhelmed but instead have inspired you.

3. Take Photographs

First, connect, breathe, open, and love unconditionally.

Suggested Materials
- Phone camera or digital camera

Time: fifteen to thirty minutes

Take a walk in your neighborhood, in a park, or any other stimulating setting. This can be a wonderful morning routine or needed break in the middle of a day. As you move, notice what is catching your eye. Is it a line or shape? Is it a texture or a shadow? Is it a flower, plant, or tree? Perhaps the clouds or the landscape?

Using your digital phone, take fifteen to twenty photos. Yesterday at the beach, I fell in love with the footprints of dogs, humans, and then the small sandpipers. Today, it was a rose from an old thorny bush. Taking photographs can become a wonderful hobby to enrich what you see. It can also give you material for your drawings and paintings.

4. Experiment with Line Drawing

First, connect, breathe, open, and love unconditionally.

Suggested Materials

- Pencil or pencil set

Time: fifteen to thirty minutes

Drawing is a wonderful exercise to do in your morning quiet time when you are just waking up. You can tell your critical mind, "I'm just drawing a line." Then ask it to relax.

You can also draw six one- to two-inch squares on your paper, and then draw within them. Somehow having a confined small space gives you permission just to practice. You can do a number of these in your lined dowsing journal or choose another blank journal to draw in.

You can do simple line drawings from the photos you took or draw what you love in your own home—perhaps a tea or coffee cup, a vase, flowers, or a plant. When my cat, Pangea, was with me, I practiced drawing her. You are attempting with a simple graphite pencil to capture the essence of a three-dimensional object, not the object itself. Try to draw what you see in front of you, not what your mind sees. Do not erase, just draw. This exercise also helps your hand and eye coordination.

5. Draw What You Love Outside

First, connect, breathe, open, and love unconditionally.

Suggested Materials

- Pencils, pens, colored pencils, and drawing set
- 8" × 8" or 12" × 12" watercolor paper

Time: twenty to thirty minutes

You can experiment with the pencils in your new set. Play with them and discover which ones are soft and hard, and what the different lines, thin or thick, look like. You can create a little chart so you get familiar with the lines each pencil makes.

Now, take your kit and a chair outside to a garden area if it's the right season, or sit by a window if it's snowing outside. What do you notice? What is attracting your attention? You can draw in your squares or use the whole sheet of paper in your drawing notebook. Play with your new set of pencils. Drawing can be incorporated into your morning quiet time. It's such a sweet way to start the day. Or such a great break in the afternoon, to get you out in the garden of life.

6. Uncover and Rid Yourself of Negative Beliefs and Blocks

First, connect, breathe, open, and love unconditionally.

Suggested Materials

- Paper to recycle
- Dark pencil, ink, or charcoal
- Dark paint

Time: five to ten minutes

Sketch a picture of your blocks. You can draw them as a person, thing, blob, or as an actual block with more detail. My blocks come out usually looking like blobs of black pencil or dark paint. I let the feeling of the block travel from my body, down my arm, into my pencil or brush. Sometimes, I make sounds as I do this exercise. It can be very freeing.

Does your block have arms, legs, tentacles, a big mouth, or a fierce look? Can you draw your block as a cartoon figure? Can you draw your block so it makes you laugh? What have you learned about your block? Yes, this picture should be ugly. Ugly is good. It will help you drop your self-judgment. Try to create ugly.

Afterward, clear yourself, write an affirmation, and if possible, burn the paper or tear it up and throw it away. You are now free!

7. Create an I AM Collage

First, connect, breathe, open, and love unconditionally.

Suggested Materials

- 8" × 8" or 12" × 12" watercolor paper
- Old or new photos of yourself
- Magazines
- Glue stick

Time: thirty to forty-five minutes

Now that you have rid yourself (or are in the process of releasing) your negative beliefs and blocks, it's a great time to make a beautiful image of yourself and all your glorious talents and aspects by creating a simple "I AM Collage." Make a list of what you like and love about yourself. You can also ask others what they like and love about you. Use a photo of yourself and include it in your collage. You can also look for images that will help you support a new vision of yourself. This collage can be created on the 12" × 12" watercolor paper or larger paper if you run out of room.

At one point in my life, I didn't like myself! I think I would have found it hard to do this exercise. If you are feeling regret, sadness, or anger toward yourself, write a list of grievances and ask your Higher Self and Spirit to forgive you. Then, find the opposite quality you would rather hold in your being. For instance if you have been unkind to your sibling, coworker, or spouse, create an image of you being kind, compassionate, and loving with all.

This exercise might bring up feelings! That's good. You're becoming more self-aware and growing into your future self. Share with friends and release!

See the book *Soul Collage Evolving: An Intuitive Collage Process for Self-Discovery and Community* by Seena B. Frost.

8. Play with Finger Painting

First, connect, breathe, open, and love unconditionally.

Suggested Materials
- 8" × 8" or 12" × 12" watercolor paper
- Acrylic paints or watercolors
- Gloves if you don't want to get your fingers colorful
- Paper towels
- Water container

Time: fifteen minutes

After organizing and purchasing your materials, aren't you excited to use them? Today, we are going to start by finger painting. Yes, we'll be using our ten digits in amazing ways.

Lock the door if needed. No one is watching. Turn on music if you prefer. Now, put five dabs of color on your palette. Dip you first finger into the paint. Doesn't that feel good? Now transfer it to the paper. See how many ways you can use your first finger. Then you can use another finger with the same color. Just play with the colors.

Go on to the next sheet of paper. Try a different color, a different finger. Try tapping your fingers in a rhythmic way. Turn up the music. Do a little dance. Continue to paint. Watch the color, your fingers. See how many different ways you can use your fingers and how many patterns you can create. See what your fingers can do. Let go.

Go to the next sheet of paper. Can you combine colors? Do you want to draw something that is in your environment with your fingers? A jar? A paintbrush, a bottle of acrylic, a flower? A lamp? Just practice and have fun. Now, didn't that exercise make you laugh?

9. Make a Dream Collage

First, connect, breathe, open, and love unconditionally.

Suggested Materials

- 8" × 8" or 12" × 12" watercolor paper
- Magazines
- Glue stick
- Scissors

Time: forty-five minutes

I have been using dream boards or vision boards for thirty or more years—beginning since I first took an afternoon Unity Church workshop. I've always loved creating dream boards because they help uncover and clarify what I truly desire . . . and they work! I have used them to manifest every material thing, from a new car to a European trip.

Did you know that it was Picasso who first began using collage in his art? Somehow, that elevated this art process for me.

Three years after the death of my husband, when I was a stressed single mom, I created a vision board around an image of a lit tunnel I found in a magazine. Although the tunnel was lit, it was still a tunnel. I desperately wanted to be on my way to my next, best big dream. For another collage, I had pictures of France, Greece, and Italy—wonderful places to visit. A few weeks later, surprise, in an email there was an offer of a twelve-day cruise on a brand-new Italian ship that sailed from Greece and around the Mediterranean, and across the Atlantic, and included airfare for $1,400. The catch? It was leaving in three weeks. On that trip, I disembarked on the French Rivera and took a train into Monaco. When I got off the train and looked around, I was in the lit tunnel from the photo on my collage!

What is your dream? Take twenty minutes to rip (a type of collage that can produce fun paper results) or cut images from magazines. Your local library often has discarded magazines. It is helpful if you want to travel to use travel magazines, or if you want to manifest a dream house to have *Sunset* or *House Beautiful* magazines.

Then create a collage. You can use your 12" × 12" watercolor paper for a background or bigger poster board paper. Move the images around until you are satisfied with your design. Use a glue stick, rather than liquid glue, because it is less messy and allows you to pick up your images and rearrange your collage if need be. Create an affirmation to affix to the front or back of your collage that supports your dream. After completing your project, put it in a prominent place that you see, and declare your affirmation out loud when you see it.

If your dream doesn't materialize quickly, continue to ask the angels to arrange the details of your future plan. Sometimes I have waited years. But when my dream materialized, it was better than I could have hoped.

See *Visioning* by Lucia Capacchione.

10. Explore with Color, Foam, and Paintbrushes

First, connect, breathe, open, and love unconditionally.

Suggested Materials

- 8" × 8" or 12" × 12" watercolor paper
- Foam brushes
- Paintbrush set
- Acrylic paints

Time: thirty to forty-five minutes

Turn on music to help lighten you up. Use a piece of watercolor paper, and dab a few dots of paint to become your color palette. Intuitively pick a foam or paintbrush, and dip in a color of your choice. Now, see how many different marks you can make with different brushes using different colors:

- Make little light lines by pressing gently.
- Paint thicker lines by pressing harder.
- Make dots with the tip of the brush.
- Make bigger dots by twirling your brush.
- Paint a word that comes to mind.

- Pick up a larger brush. Let go and go bolder.
- Go have a cup of tea! Dance a little and let your painting dry. (You can also use a hair dryer.)
- Then pick up a small paintbrush to create details.
- Stand back and ask, "What does this painting need?"
- What do you see in your painting? What is it saying to you?

11. Mix and Play with Paint

First, connect, breathe, open, and love unconditionally.

Suggested Materials

- 8" × 8" or 12" × 12" watercolor paper
- Foam brushes
- Paintbrush set
- Acrylic paints

Time: thirty to forty-five minutes

I am still amazed that I can take two colors and make a new color. For instance, blue and yellow produce green! I know it all has to do with physics and color theory (first written about by Newton), but hey, it seems like magic. If you mix red and blue, you get violet; yellow and red become orange. You can add white to magenta to make pink, my favorite color. If you have a set of colors, this is the time to play with them. Now look and see what colors you love. Create a painting with them!

Make a variety of marks. Paint something you love from your environment. Let the painting dry and add details using smaller paintbrushes.

12. Create an Income Streams Collage

First, connect, breathe, open, and love unconditionally.

Suggested Materials

- Images
- Magazines

- Photographs
- Watercolor paper 12" × 12" or other stiff paper for the back-ground of the collage

Time: thirty to forty-five minutes

It's time to create a collage about income streams. You can first dowse the Income Streams Chart (26). Answer the suggested questions. Are there any new surprises?

Draw or paint a river with flowing multiple tributaries that run through your paper. Again, spend twenty minutes ripping out images and words from magazines. (It's again helpful to have magazines that represent your artistic area and money magazines, such as *Forbes*, *The Economist*, or *Kiplinger's*.)

As you cut or tear, let your inner critic rest, and *think big*. If you had an endless source of resources, time, and talent, what income streams would you create? Note: God/Goddess loves to help us with dreams. The Creator didn't just materialize one flower, but a million varieties.

Now, spend time arranging your collage. After finishing, ask, "What is the primary message that my collage is attempting to give me?" Write your message on another piece of paper and add it to your collage. Or you can write it on the back. Again, post your collage and see your income streams multiply.

13. Discover Intuitive Painting with Collage

First, connect, breathe, open, and love unconditionally.

Suggested Materials
- 8" × 8" and/or 12" × 12" watercolor paper
- Acrylic paints
- Foam brushes
- Paintbrushes
- Acrylic pens
- Images from printed materials
- Glue stick
- Liquitex gloss acrylic fluid medium and varnish
- Water container

Time: thirty to forty-five minutes

I must admit I've already tricked you! You've already begun to create intuitive paintings in the last few painting exercises. I just want you to keep going and play with all the materials and processes you've been using.

We're going to create three to six paintings with three different layers or more. Turn on your music. Time for action and exploration. Set up your painting table with a covering for your painting surface. Arrange your materials. Lay out three smaller 8" × 8" papers and have your larger 12" × 12" at hand.

1. Background for painting—This is such a fun way to start, because with acrylic you can get loose on the first layer. You can use your foam brushes, paintbrushes, and fingers. Let your brushes and fingers find a rhythm with the music. You don't need to be making anything at all at this stage. It's all about movement and enjoying the colors. What color are you craving? Go back and forth between the three pieces of paper. If you've completed layer one on one sheet, you can move to another sheet while the paints dry on the first one. After you finish, take a photo of each painting. You will be covering up some of this, so it helps to let go of what you've already painted.

2. Add a word or a phrase to your layer, naming what you are feeling as you're painting. Use words such as *joy, excitement, grace, love, abundance,* or any of the words or phrases you love. Sometimes it's *anger, jealousy, hatred,* and a little dark. But by naming what you feel, you are releasing the difficult emotion and unblocking. You can always paint over it later. If you want to write more, turn the painting over and write. Just make sure your painting is dried.

3. Second layer—Just spend some time looking at your little painting. What does it need? What would add more variety—a unique mark, a contrasting color, a harmonizing color? Ask your painting what it wants you to paint. Is there something inspiring in your workspace? A flower? A tree outside your window? A shape? Or a vase?

Is a face or a body coming through your painting? Do you see the beginning of an animal?

4. When it's dry, use acrylic pens to make more details on your painting.

5. Does your painting need a bit of collage? You can use a glue stick or the gloss acrylic medium and varnish to adhere the image to the painting and to coat your paintings after they have dried.

6. Explore and have fun!

This is just a beginning. For more ideas, see the following sources:

Books:

Brave Intuitive Painting by Flora Bowley
Creative Revolution by Flora Bowley
Life, Paint and Passion: Reclaiming the Magic of Spontaneous Expression, by Michele Cassou and Steward Cubley
Rise Above by Whitney Freya
Collage Workbook by Randel Plowman
Project Collage by Bev Speight

My Favorite Online Art Teachers and Classes:

Flora Bowley at *florabowley.com*
Tracy Verdugo at *tracyverdugo.com*

Just opening Flora Bowley's book and going to her website will inspire you; and visiting Tracy Verdugo's website will brighten any day.

14. Devise a Success Collage

Suggested Materials
- Fluid watercolor paper 12" × 12"
- Golden paints
- Paintbrushes
- Magazines

Time: forty-five minutes

Paint a background for your collage. It can be just one color or multiple colors. Perhaps it is sky blue, bright yellow, or . . . Then let it dry.

Spend a few moments contemplating when you were successful in the past. How did that feel? Were you elated, giddy, a little frightened? Now take that feeling and project it into the future. What is the inward feeling of success you want to create for yourself? What is the outward manifestation of that success? An art show, a music performance, a book contract? Money? Lots of money? Money can be thought of as spiritual substance turned into coin, green bills, and sums and zeros of money in your bank account. You certainly have worked hard and deserve financial success too.

Create a collage based on your Intuitive Action Plan and the success you crave and want to see. Include positive words, an affirmation, or your vision statement from your Intuitive Action Plan in the collage.

15. Gather Your Work Together

We have completed many art exercises in this book! To honor all the work you've completed, put it together in a folder, your sketch book, or a colorful box; or create a larger mosaic vision board that you can refer to often to spur you onward to your dreams.

If you dowse every day, you will be become a much better diviner, and if you do an art exercise each day, your art will improve in leaps and bounds. Even giving yourself fifteen minutes to draw, collage, and paint can enhance and open your creative senses.

Doing the exercises in this book might spur you to buy a book or take an online or in-person art class. See the suggested reading and web resources throughout the chapter.

Most importantly, keep on divining, journaling, and making art!

CHAPTER 16

Start Your Own Divine Creativity Cluster

Cluster together like stars.

—HENRY MILLER, American writer and artist

Watching others learn to dowse is still stirring—when students hold the pendulum and it moves of its own accord, when they receive the *yes/no* signal and then learn to use the pendulum with the Intuitive Creativity Charts. I can see a door in the mind of students open to their innate gift of divining. Now they have the tools and a self-coaching/coaching method to guide and explore their creative lives. They will soon have the profound ability to help others do this too.

I do love giving classes. Up until 2020 and the COVID-19 pandemic, these classes were in person and in my loft at the Tannery Artist Lofts. I always wanted my students to feel safe, enjoy themselves, learn, open up, and grow. We have such a wonderful and fun time helping each other, and are always amazed at the spiritual energy, love, and deep friendships that are made. By combining all three activities—dowsing, journaling, and art projects—students experience new insights about their self and life, and are helped on their creative path. The classes feel like a sacred party where we share the mystery of creativity.

After you have become proficient using the pendulum and the Intuitive Creativity Charts, you may want to create your own cluster of like-minded people who want to learn to dowse, journal, and play together! If you are so inclined to teach, this chapter is for you. It's taking your skill to another level, because when you teach, you will learn the finer points and have the pleasure of giving to another the gift of creativity and dowsing.

Teaching may be a little intimidating at first, but I will give you a very short course. Preparation is essential so that when you are with students, you are able to focus on them, and not on all the details! Just like teaching elementary students, you will have to have agreements and boundaries with your students, and refocus the group when they get off track. I like to read the following guidelines at every class, especially in the beginning.

Divine Creative Cluster Guidelines

You may want to write your own guiding principles with your group. Reading the rules at the beginning of the meeting helps reinforce them, and then everyone knows what to expect.

- Our collective intention is to create a place of safety and acceptance for each member to feel the loving and healing power of Spirit.
- We will practice listening and mindfulness while each speaks their truth.
- Cross talk will be minimal. We understand each person is on their creative journey and inwardly knows what is best for them.
- Loving feedback, when requested, will be given to enrich the person, never to weaken them.
- Each person sharing will know what they say is held in confidence.
- There will be equal time for each member.
- We will make the group safe and comfortable for all.
- Love is our code. Spirit is our answer to all our creativity needs.

The following are insights about how you can structure the class. Each class will be different, but if everyone knows what the makeup of the class is beforehand, then people can settle into the rhythm. It's also important to give a short break, as people will need a moment for a bite to eat and a sip of tea. Also, students can get to know each other during this time.

Structure for the Divine Creative Group

- Meet once a week, every other week, or once a month. Once you have set a time to meet, it's important to keep the commitment and meet regularly.

- Especially when beginning, you might want to invite only like-minded friends who will be open to new ideas, dowsing, journaling, and doing fun art projects.

- Send out a reminder email to the group with the date and time and what to bring for the upcoming class—for instance, a pendulum, notebook, and art supplies.

- Create an agenda or outline to keep yourself on track, including making any announcements.

- The studio, classroom, or your living room should be clean and comfortable. It's important that the trash is taken out.

- Clear the room using your pendulum. Sometimes, I also clear the participants before they come!

- Flowers add a touch of grace.

- Prepare tea, water, and healthy snacks if you want.

- Before people arrive, prepare yourself. Ground and ask the Creative Spirit to join the group and any other spirit guides you may want to invite.

- Have an open, playful attitude. Having fun relaxes you, engages both sides of the brain, and lifts you to a higher vibration. It also opens the subconscious and helps us integrate all parts of our being. Remember, our Creator is infinitely joyful.

- To begin, light a candle and say a simple prayer, thanking the Creator and other Guides for joining the group.

- The facilitator or another member of the group can lead a grounding meditation. Often many of us are ungrounded, especially because of our busy lives—unconnected with the earth, our bodies, and our spiritual support. It can be helpful to do the Grounding and Chakra Meditations in the beginning. Both meditations are found in Chapter 4.

- Read the guidelines (see the preceding section) for the Divine Creativity Cluster; this is a simple way to reinforce the intention of the group and make sure everyone understands the ground rules.

- Individual member's check-in—When leading groups, I like to give people the opportunity to tell about what is happening in their lives. This gives them a chance to become present if anything exciting is taking place or if there is something weighing on their minds. Usually, checking in takes three to five minutes per person, and sometimes you have to remind the group that this check-in is short. This is a great time for all to practice mindful listening, focusing on the speaker, but refraining from giving feedback. This also allows the speaker the freedom to say what is on their mind without feeling judged.

- Cluster activities—You can cover one chapter of this book, which helps new pendulum dowsers, or two chapters a week, which is a good pace for a more experienced group.

- In closing the group, you can stand and create a small circle. I always say a short closing prayer, and others in the group chime in with their thoughts or prayers too. If the group is large, I ask for one word representing their experience in the group. In the end, it's almost like we've created a shared poem, and we close the sacred circle.

Let the class know what is planned for a two-hour meeting. This is how I divide the time:

- Opening Activities: five minutes
- Check-in: twenty minutes
- Reading and Reviewing the Chapter: twenty minutes
- Break: ten minutes
- Dowsing: thirty minutes
- Art Activities: thirty minutes
- Closing: five minutes
- Homework: Review the upcoming chapter, write journaling prompts, and practice using the pendulum with the charts.

New Groups

When starting a new group, people will have different levels of expertise. Some will be brand new to pendulum dowsing, and others will have much more experience. Each class will vary in their needs and goals. Some will want to cover different topics, and some suggested art activities will appeal to some groups and not others.

I like to find out in the first meeting what everyone's needs are and to check in periodically during the class to see if their needs are being met. Everyone wants to be heard, respected, valued, and understood; patience and tolerance with a large dose of compassion are vital.

The class does not have to do all the Experiential Exercises; the teacher can choose how many to do and what to cover for each class.

Journaling

I like to assign the Journaling Prompts for homework, when students can quietly reflect on their own during their morning quiet time. Then, during the check-in period, see if they want to share insights from their journaling process.

Dowsing

You can also read parts of the chapters out loud, review the processes, and complete the worksheets. Everyone can practice, ask questions, and learn the multiple ways to use the charts. The teacher can demonstrate how to do Intuitive Creativity Coaching using the charts and worksheets and forms found in Chapters 13 and 14. Please feel free to copy all worksheets, forms, and charts if you want an enlarged set of charts.

Creative Activities

Set up your art table before the class. You will introduce the activity and perhaps have a sample that you have previously done. Keep it simple. It's nice to put on relaxing music to set the mood. If people are quiet, they can focus on the art activity. This is for entertainment and exploration. Encourage your students with their first attempts.

At the end of the process, you can have "show and tell." And students can answer questions such as

- How did you feel when you were going through this process?
- Would you give your process a name?
- What is your art piece telling you?
- What other insights do you have?

Doing these activities is not about perfection, but process. If people want to apologize for their work, they must say out loud three times, "I'm so sexy." (Stolen from an Improvisation class long ago!) Then everyone laughs and we are reminded that we are all beginners in this game.

Experienced Dowsers

After your group has read the chapters, completed the exercises, and become proficient diviners, there is a possibility your group may want to continue to meet—to review chapters, practice dowsing, give Intuitive Creativity Coaching, and do art projects. Some of my classes have continued on for years. We have explored different art activities—collage, beading, Soul Cards, watercolor mandalas, and acrylic intuitive painting. See "Bibliography and Recommended Reading" for art book "how-to" guides.

Advice for the Teacher

If you're the teacher, it is best if you work with Spirit and your Guides. I work with the angels of light and love and the archangels. It's funny, but if I'm nervous before a class, I sit down, clear myself, close my eyes, and talk to the angels just as I would friends. I say, "Are you coming? Are you here? Please help me!" Then I see them in my mind's eye sitting on the loft above my living room. I laugh, because in the twenty years I've been teaching spiritual classes, they always come.

As to my doubts, I am just human, I remind myself. But then, when I begin, it's as if I settle into my teaching and let go. Then, the powerful, sweet energy flows through me. The true teacher is Spirit. As human teachers, we are there to support the spiritual, creative activities in a conscious way.

Except when requested, you are not looking for solutions for class members. By listening well, you are helping people go within to find their own solutions and use their dowsing tools. Lean on the angels and God/Goddess instead.

Once in a while, a person wants to dominate a meeting. Usually, I give this person a responsibility, and then they can focus their energies within the group. Often it means the person does have much to share, but they are, unconsciously or not, doing it in a way that is unbalanced for the group. You can refer back to the class guidelines. If necessary, speak to this person after class. In the group, we are learning to take responsibility for ourselves, discovering our own issues and solutions, and developing our creativity. Modeling this in class is another learning experience.

Often in my clusters, even though we discuss deep issues, there is much laughter. To me, it's a sign the angels are with us and that higher forces are in play. Despite outer circumstances that might be unfolding in our lives, joking and laughing are great medicine for the soul. Laughter helps us be humble as children in the loving hands of God/Goddess.

A Maxim for the Road

You can borrow from these generous artists or write your own statement of truth. It's so important to have encouraging and powerful words guiding your way.

Farther on, and deeper in!

—HAPPI CAMPBELL, sculptor and painter

I love you (to myself).

—MARGARET NIVEN, visual artist and college teacher

Slow down and be grateful for my human life and all that I have.

—MARIA CHOMENTOWSKI, visual artist and writer

I am safe, blessed, prosperous, and abundant.

—CATHERINE SEGURSON, founding editor of the
Catamaran Literary Reader

You got this—get it done.

—SANDRA SHAMMA, singer and songwriter

Life is too short not to have fun.

—SONIA LE, fashion designer

Write terribly every day and look for what's already there.

—ELIZABETH MCKENZIE, novelist

Singing "you can do it" to the tune of "Happy Birthday" at least twice. Clearly, I need more mantras.

—PAMELA PAPAS, writer and stand-up comedian

KEEP IT MOVING. This helps me in every way. Movement creates heat, which generates life.

—JOSEPH LACOUR, spoken word poet, artist, and emcee

I remember the words of Anaïs Nin, "Art is the alchemy that turns ordinary materials into gold."

—MAGDALENA MONTAGNE, poet and poetry teacher

In Closing

Though I have not met you yet in person, I feel very close to you right at this moment as I finish this book. I see you on your own divining, creative journey. As you learn and grow, you will be able to help others become their authentic selves. By being in the creative flow with Spirit, you will, by your words and actions, be inspiring, enlivening others. Remember, this is only a beginning, but with the help of Spirit and other creatives on the path, we will live well and travel together. Happy creating and divining!

Creativity is contagious, pass it on.

—ALBERT EINSTEIN

ACKNOWLEDGMENTS

To the loving angels, generous spirit guides, and the muses who urged and sometimes drove me to write this book, thank you for your inspiration, wise words, and encouragement.

To Judika Illes, my Red Wheel/Weiser editor, who cast a spell and helped birth this book. To the Red Wheel/Weiser publishing editors, graphic artists, and staff for further bringing this book to life with all their creative talents and detailed work. To my agent, Rita Rosenkranz, who helped with the detailed contract and guided me in communications.

To Magdalena Montagne, my personal editor, coach, and lyrical poetry teacher, who read, edited, and offered support chapter by chapter. To Juanita Usher, for her purple pen and further edifying editing skills. For Pamela Papas, who reviewed the manuscript, completed all the "Paint on Your Hands" art exercises, and produced fun original art pieces. To Marion Blair, who gave me a retreat hearth to make final manuscript changes.

To the amazing Julia Cameron, creator of *The Artist's Way*, and to all my students over the last fifteen years, who shared the journey.

To my many clients, students, and readers, who ventured into the creative waters with me. Thank you for the support of my work, for purchasing my books, learning how to divine and dowse, and sharing your enthusiasm.

To Catherine Segurson, brilliant founder of the *Catamaran Literary Reader* and the Catamaran Writing Conference, who gave me a "room of my own" to write this book. To the Tannery Arts and Artspace for providing me with a creative home.

To my adult children, Danielle and Adam Torvik-Staffen, and my sisters, Laurie Carah, Therese Moldvay, and Leslie Torvik, who share this profound earth school—the highs and lows and in betweens with me.

To my new husband, Walt Froloff, inventor and much more, for his love and patience, especially during the COVID-19 pandemic and during the writing of this book.

To the following artists who were interviewed and offered their ideas and advice in this book:

Happi Campbell, artist and sculptor

Maria Chomentowski, visual artist and writer, *flickr.com/photos/mariachomentowski*

Joseph LaCour, spoken word poet, artist, and emcee, *www.josephjasonsantiagolacour.com*

Sonia Le, fashion designer: *cosmochicsc.com*

Elizabeth McKenzie, novelist, *stopthatgirl.com*

Magdalena Montagne, poet and poetry teacher, *poetrycirclewithmagdalena.com*

Margaret Niven, visual artist and college teacher, *margaretniven.com*

Pamela Papas, writer and stand-up comedian *facebook.com/pamela.papas.5*

Krista Pollock, pastry chef/baker, *www.instagram.com/pollockpastry*

Catherine Segurson, founding editor of the *Catamaran Literary Reader, catamaranliteraryreader.com*

Sandra Shamma, singer and songwriter, *facebook.com/shammamama/*

Maha Taitano, sculptor and installation artist, *instagram.com/maha_taitano/*

Dani Torvik, visual artist, *danielletorvik-staffen.squarespace.com*

Rachel Van Dessel, painter and dancer, *visualartsnetworkscc.com*

My gratitude, appreciation, and thanks to you all for sharing the journey.

BIBLIOGRAPHY AND RECOMMENDED READING

Aura and Chakras

Ambrose, Kala. *The Awakened Aura*. Woodbury, MN: Llewellyn Publications, 2011.

Bruere, Rosalyn L. *Wheels of Light*, New York, NY: Atria Books, 1994.

Myss, Caroline. *Anatomy of the Spirit*. New York, NY: Crown Publishers, 1996.

Art Books (How-To Guides)

Apter, Seth. *The Mixed-Media Artist*. Cincinnati, OH: North Light Books, 2013.

Beam, Mary Todd. *Celebrate Your Creative Self*. Cincinnati, OH: North Light Books, 2003.

Bowley, Flora. *Brave Intuitive Painting*. Beverly, MA: Quarto Publishing Group, 2012.

_____. *Creative Revolution*. Beverly, MA: Quarto Publishing Group, 2016.

_____. *The Art of Aliveness*. San Antonio, TX: Hierophant Publishing, 2021.

Freya, Whitney. *Rise Above*. Lyme, CT: Flower of Life Press, 2017.

Frost, Seena B. *Soul Collage*. Santa Cruz, CA: Hanford Mead Publishers, 2001.

Marine, Carol. *Daily Painting*. New York, NY: Penguin Random House, 2014.

Norvick, Linda. *The Painting Path*. Woodstock, VT: Skylight Paths, 2007.

Plowman, Randel. *Collage Workbook*. New York, NY: Sterling Publishers, 2012.

Speight, Bev. *Project Collage*. London, UK: Hatchette, 2019.

Business

Beam, Lisa Sonara. *The Creative Entrepreneur.* Beverly, MA: Quayside Publishing Group, 2008.

Congdon, Lisa. *Art Inc.* San Francisco, CA: Chronicle Books, 2014.

Lang, Cay. *Taking the Leap.* San Francisco, CA: Chronicle Books, 1998.

MacNeil, Natalie. *The Conquer Kit.* New York, NY: Penguin Random House, 2015.

Creativity Coaching

Bolles, Richard. *What Color Is Your Parachute?, Rev. ed.* Emeryville, CA: Ten Speed Press, 2019.

Maisel, Eric. *Fearless Creating.* New York, NY: Penguin Putnam Inc., 1995.

McGuinness, Mark. *21 Insights for 21st Century Creatives.* United Kingdom: Lateral Action Books, 2019.

Stolzfus, Tony. *Coaching Questions.* Virginia Beach, VA: Author, 2008.

Creativity Process and Recovery

Cameron, Julia. *The Artist's Way.* New York, NY: G. P. Putnam's Sons, 1992.

Cassou, Michele, and Cubley, Stewart. *Life, Paint and Passion.* New York, NY: Penguin, Putnam, Inc., 1995.

Cornell, Judith. *Drawing the Light Within.* New York, NY: Simon & Schuster, 1990.

Faia, Michele. *Art in My Heart.* Aptos, CA: Michele Faia, 2007.

Fox, Matthew. *Creativity, Where the Divine and Human Meet.* New York, NY: Penguin Putnam, 2002.

Nordby, Jacob. *Blessed Are the Weird.* Boise, ID: Manifesto Publishing House, 2016.

_____. *The Creative Cure.* San Antonio, TX: Hierophant Publishing, 2021.

Pearce, Lucy. *Creatrix, She Who Makes.* East Cork, Ireland: Womancraft Publishing, 2019.

Pressfield, Steven. *The War of Art.* New York, NY: Warner Books, 2002.

Tharp, Twyla. *The Creative Habit.* New York, NY: Simon & Schuster, Inc. 2003.

Communication

Rosenberg, Marshall. *Nonviolent Communication: A Language of Life.* Encinitas, CA: Puddle Dancer Press, 2005.

Dreams and Visioning

Capacchione, Lucia. *Visioning.* New York, NY: Penguin Putnam, Inc., 2000.

Hiller, Margaret, and Hiller, David. *Dare to Dream.* Ashland, OR: Heart Dream Press, 2002.

Moss, Robert. *Growing Big Dreams.* Novato, CA: New World Library 2020.

Healing

Loyd, Alexander, with Johnson, Ben. *The Healing Code.* New York, NY: Hachette Book Group, 2010.

Myss, Caroline. *Anatomy of the Spirit.* New York, NY: Crown Publishers, 1996.

Intuition

Peirce, Penny. *The Intuitive Way.* New York, NY: Simon & Schuster, Inc., Atria, Beyond Words, 2010.

Meditation

Kornfield, Jack. *Meditation for Beginners.* Boulder, CO: Sounds True, 2004.

Nature

MacGregor, Catriona. *Partnering with Nature.* New York, NY: Simon & Schuster, Inc., Atria, and Beyond Words, 2010.

Other

Course in Miracles. Tiburon, CA: Foundation for Inner Peace, 1975.

Gilbert, Elizabeth. *Eat, Pray, Love*, New York, NY: Penguin Random House, 2007.

Howkins, John. *The Creative Economy.* New York, NY: Penguin, 2013.

Miro, Shaheen. *The Lunar Nomad Oracle.* Newburyport, MA: Red Wheel/Weiser, 2018.

Ness, Patrick. *A Monster Calls.* Somerville, MA: Candlewick Press, 2013.

Strayed, Cheryl. *Brave Enough: A Mini Instruction Manual for the Soul.* New York, NY: Alfred A. Knopf, 2015.

Pendulum Dowsing

Bird, Christopher. *The Divining Hand.* New York, NY: E. P. Dutton, 1979.

Brown, Elizabeth. *Dowsing, The Ultimate Guide for the 21st Century.* United Kingdom: Hay House, 2010.

Detzler, Robert E. *The Freedom Path.* Snohomish, WA: Snohomish Publishing Company, Inc., 1996.

————. *Soul Re-Creation: Developing Your Cosmic Potential.* Redmond, WA: SRC Publishing, revised 1999.

Staffen, Joan Rose. *The Book of Pendulum Healing.* Newburyport, MA: Red Wheel/Weiser, 2019.

————. *Divination & Action.* Santa Cruz, CA: CreateSpace Platform, 2012.

————. *Divination & Joy.* Santa Cruz, CA: CreateSpace Platform, 2012.

Webster, Richard. *Pendulum Magic for Beginners.* St. Paul, MN: Llewellyn Publications, 2005.

Sales and Marketing

Caballo, Frances. *Avoid Social Media Time Suck.* Santa Rosa, CA: Act Communications, 2014.

————. *Social Media Just for Writers.* Santa Rosa, CA: Act Communications, 2016.

Carey, Brainard. *Sell Online Like a Creative Genius.* New York, NY: Allworth Press, 2019.

Hyatt, Michael. *Platform: Get Noticed in a Noisy World.* Nashville, TN: Thomas Nelson, Inc., 2012.

Katz, Christina. *Get Known Before the Deal.* Blue Ash, OH: Writer's Digest Books, 2008.

Success

Brophy, Maria. *Art Money Success.* San Clemente, CA: Sons of the Sea, Inc., 2017.

Clancy, Andrew B. *The Success Gurus.* New York, NY: Penguin Group, 2011.

Writing

Amir, Nina. *The Author Training Manual.* Blue Ash, OH: Writer's Digest Books, 2014.

Conner, Janet. *Writing Down Your Soul.* Newburyport, MA: Red Wheel/Weiser, 2008.

Fox, John. *Poetic Medicine,* New York, NY: Penguin, Putnam, 1997.

Goldberg, Natalie. *Writing Down the Bones.* Boston, MA: Shambhala, 2016.

Lamont, Ann. *Bird by Bird.* New York, NY: Knopf Doubleday Publishing Group, 1995.

Rosenfeld, Jordan. *A Writer's Guide to Persistence.* Blue Ash, OH: Writer's Digest Books, 2015.

APPENDIX

The Thirty-Three Intuitive Creativity Charts

Before beginning, center yourself, take a few deep breaths, and ask using your pendulum:

- Am I working with High Self?
- Are my answers accurate?

    If no, keep clearing until you are ready.

If you are working with another person, always ask first:

- Do I have permission to work with this person?
- Is this for the highest good for this person?

    If the answer is no, you can always say a prayer for them, and place them in Spirit's hands.

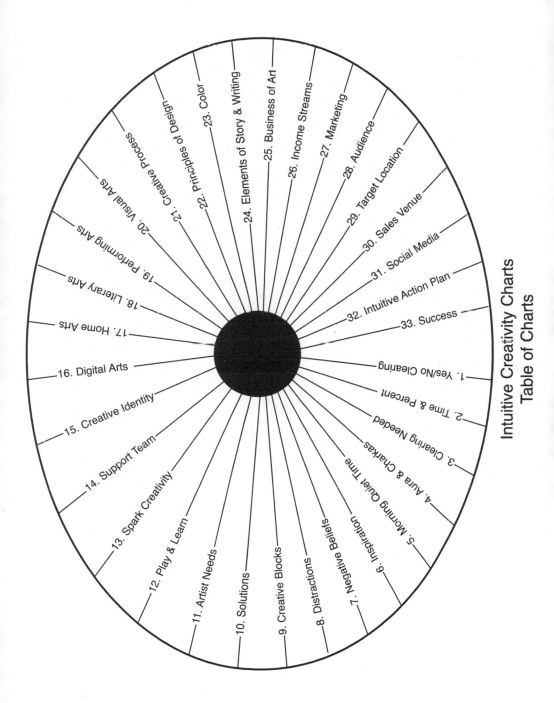

Intuitive Creativity Charts
Table of Charts

1. Yes/No Clearing
2. Time & Percent
3. Clearing Needed
4. Aura & Chakras
5. Morning Quiet Time
6. Inspiration
7. Negative Beliefs
8. Distractions
9. Creative Blocks
10. Solutions
11. Artist Needs
12. Play & Learn
13. Spark Creativity
14. Support Team
15. Creative Identity
16. Digital Arts
17. Home Arts
18. Literary Arts
19. Performing Arts
20. Visual Arts
21. Creative Process
22. Principles of Design
23. Color
24. Elements of Story & Writing
25. Business of Art
26. Income Streams
27. Marketing
28. Audience
29. Target Location
30. Sales Venue
31. Social Media
32. Intuitive Action Plan
33. Success

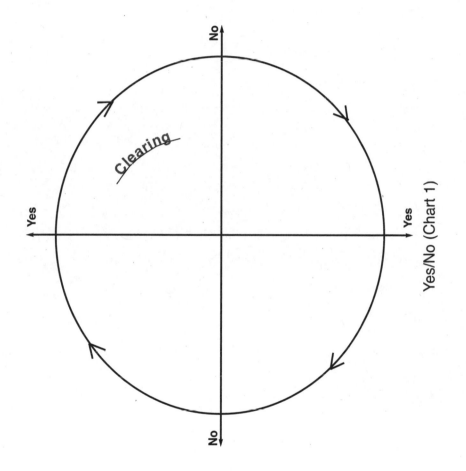

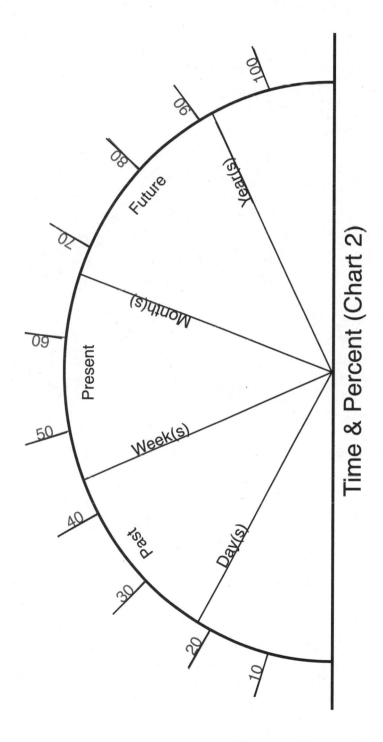

Time & Percent (Chart 2)

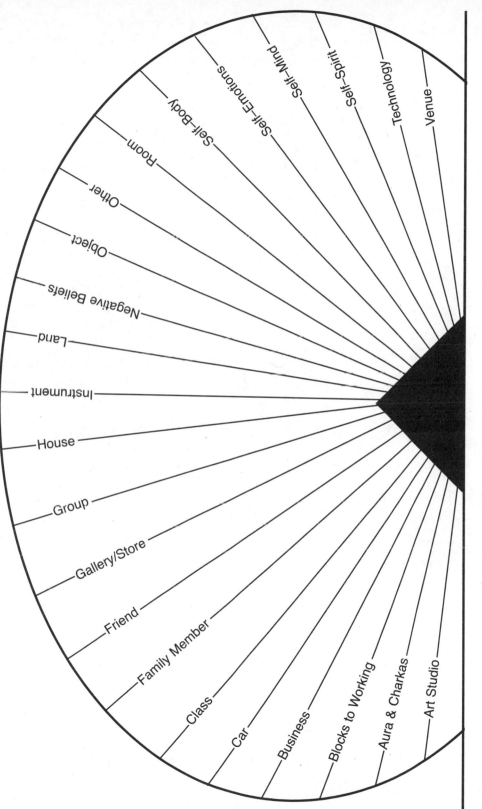

Clearing Needed (Chart 3)

- Venue
- Technology
- Self-Spirit
- Self-Mind
- Self-Emotions
- Self-Body
- Room
- Other
- Object
- Negative Beliefs
- Land
- Instrument
- House
- Group
- Gallery/Store
- Friend
- Family Member
- Class
- Car
- Business
- Blocks to Working
- Aura & Charkas
- Art Studio

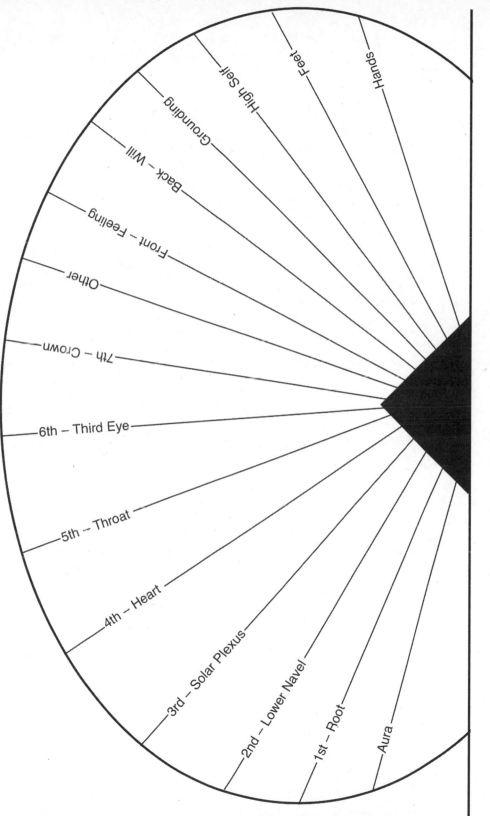

Aura & Chakras (Chart 4)

Hands

Feet

High Self

Grounding

Back – Will

Front – Feeling

Other

7th – Crown

6th – Third Eye

5th – Throat

4th – Heart

3rd – Solar Plexus

2nd – Lower Navel

1st – Root

Aura

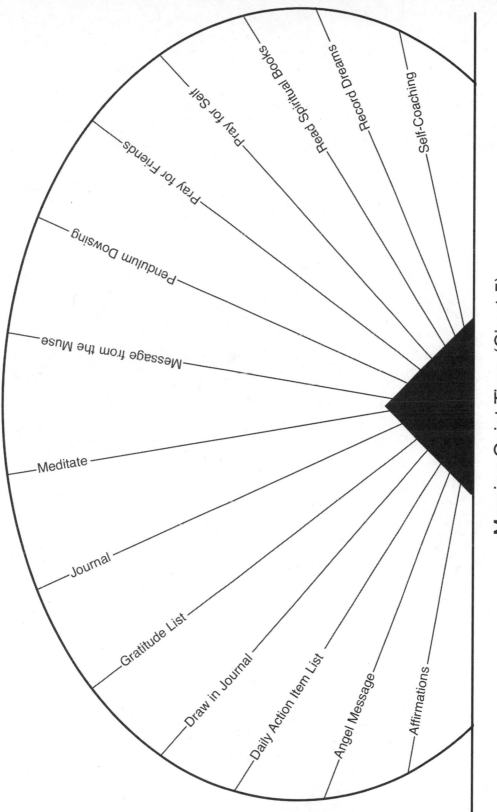

Morning Quiet Time (Chart 5)

Self-Coaching
Record Dreams
Read Spiritual Books
Pray for Self
Pray for Friends
Pendulum Dowsing
Message from the Muse
Meditate
Journal
Gratitude List
Draw in Journal
Daily Action Item List
Angel Message
Affirmations

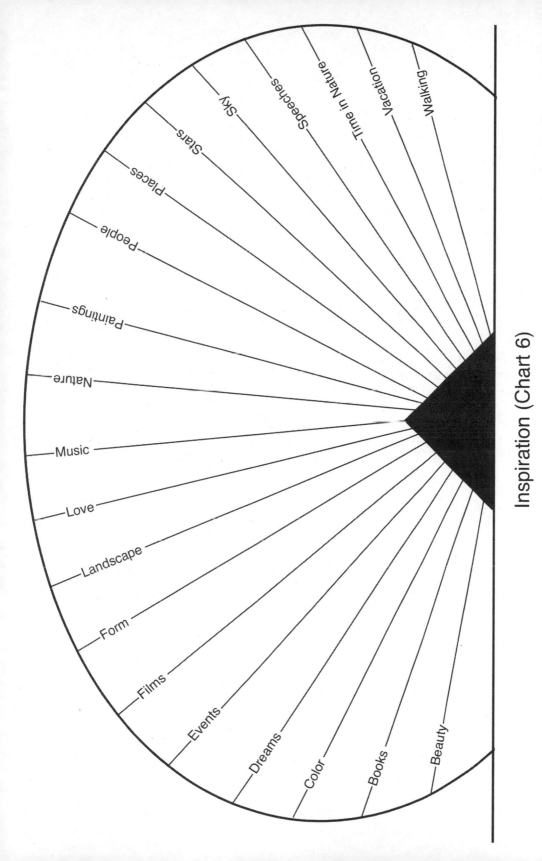

Inspiration (Chart 6)

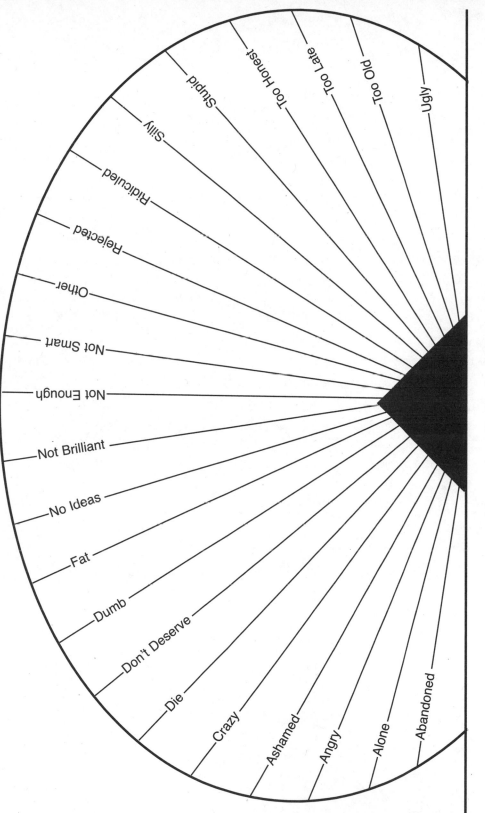

Negative Beliefs (Chart 7)

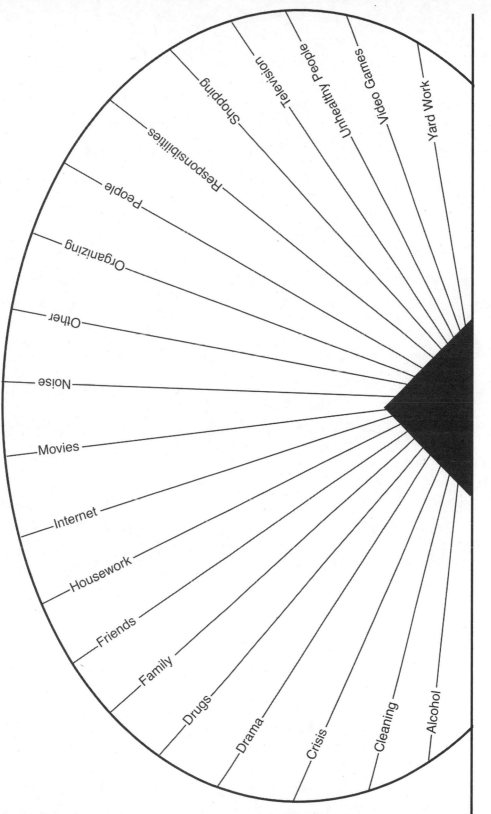

Distractions (Chart 8)

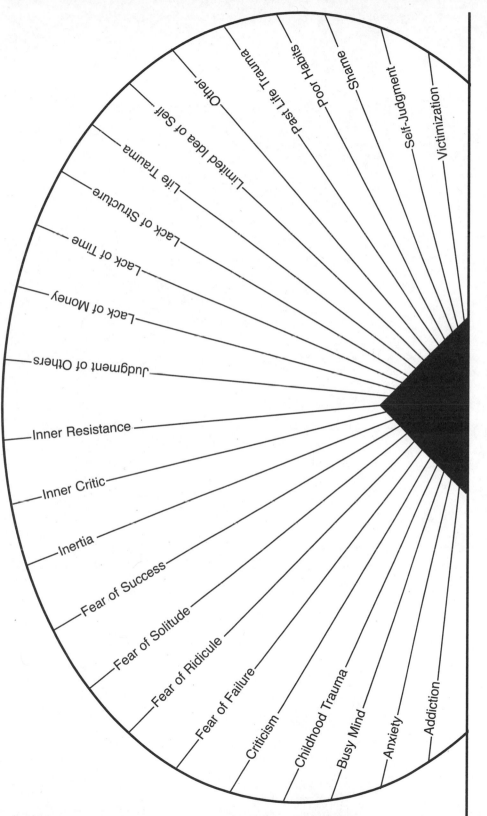

Creative Blocks (Chart 9)

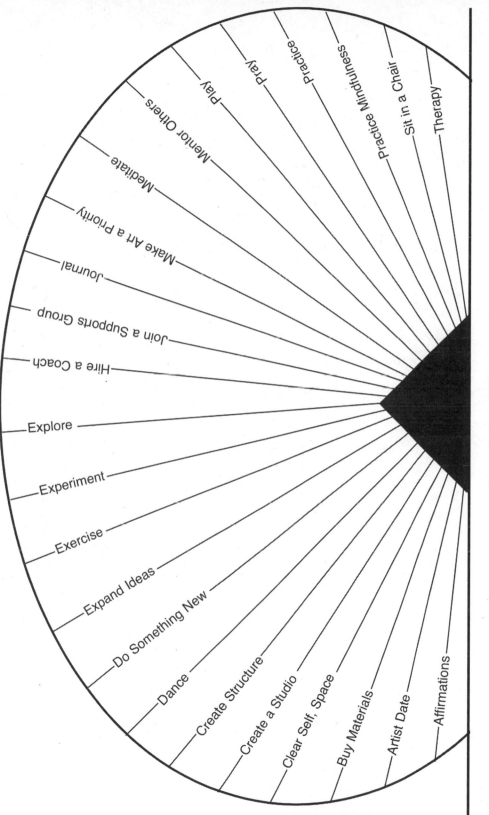

Solutions (Chart 10)

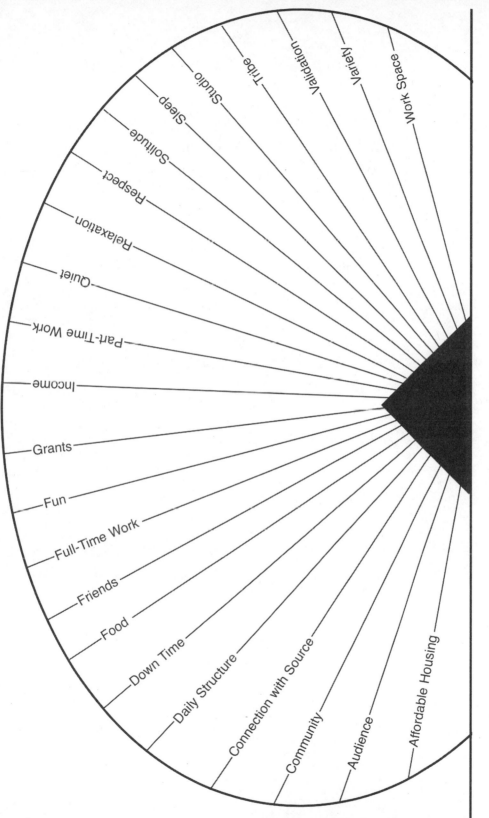

Artist Needs (Chart 11)

Work Space
Variety
Validation
Tribe
Studio
Sleep
Solitude
Respect
Relaxation
Quiet
Part-Time Work
Income
Grants
Fun
Full-Time Work
Friends
Food
Down Time
Daily Structure
Connection with Source
Community
Audience
Affordable Housing

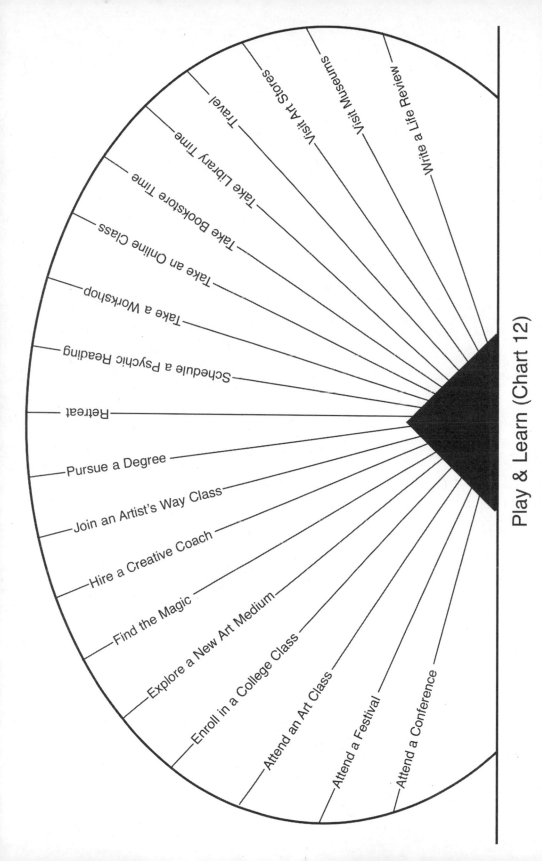

Play & Learn (Chart 12)

Write a Life Review
Visit Museums
Visit Art Stores
Travel
Take Library Time
Take Bookstore Time
Take an Online Class
Take a Workshop
Schedule a Psychic Reading
Retreat
Pursue a Degree
Join an Artist's Way Class
Hire a Creative Coach
Find the Magic
Explore a New Art Medium
Enroll in a College Class
Attend an Art Class
Attend a Festival
Attend a Conference

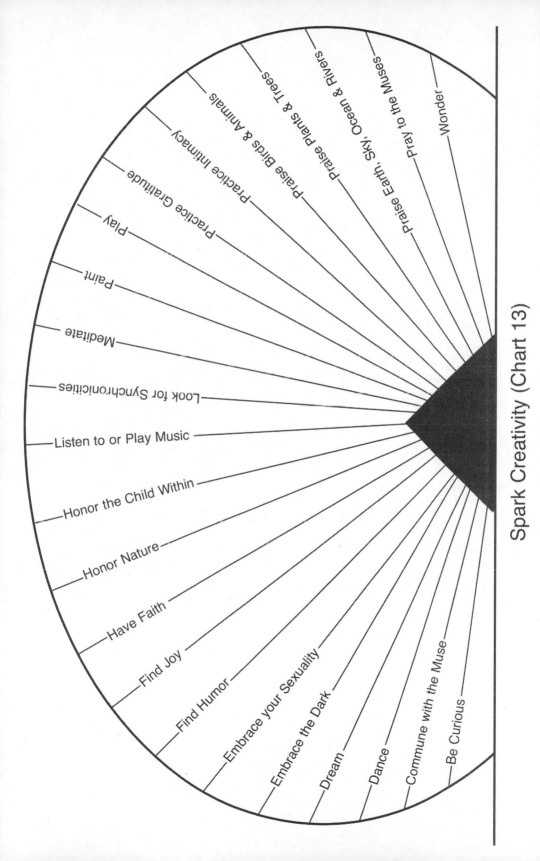

Spark Creativity (Chart 13)

Wonder
Pray to the Muses
Praise Earth, Sky, Ocean & Rivers
Praise Plants & Trees
Praise Birds & Animals
Practice Intimacy
Practice Gratitude
Play
Paint
Meditate
Look for Synchronicities
Listen to or Play Music
Honor the Child Within
Honor Nature
Have Faith
Find Joy
Find Humor
Embrace your Sexuality
Embrace the Dark
Dream
Dance
Commune with the Muse
Be Curious

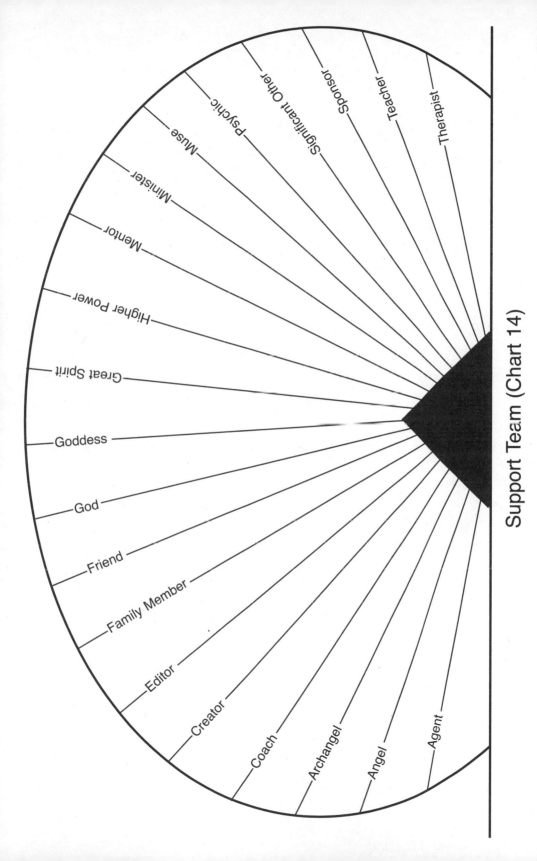

Support Team (Chart 14)

Therapist
Teacher
Sponsor
Significant Other
Psychic
Muse
Minister
Mentor
Higher Power
Great Spirit
Goddess
God
Friend
Family Member
Editor
Creator
Coach
Archangel
Angel
Agent

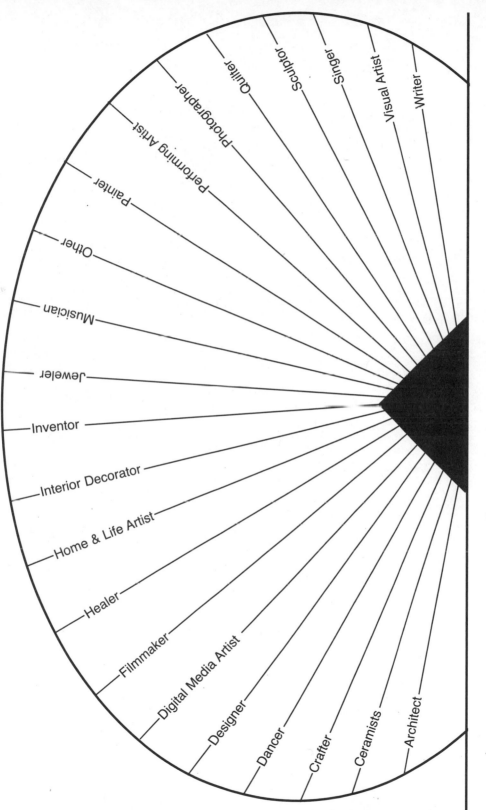

Creative Identity (Chart 15)

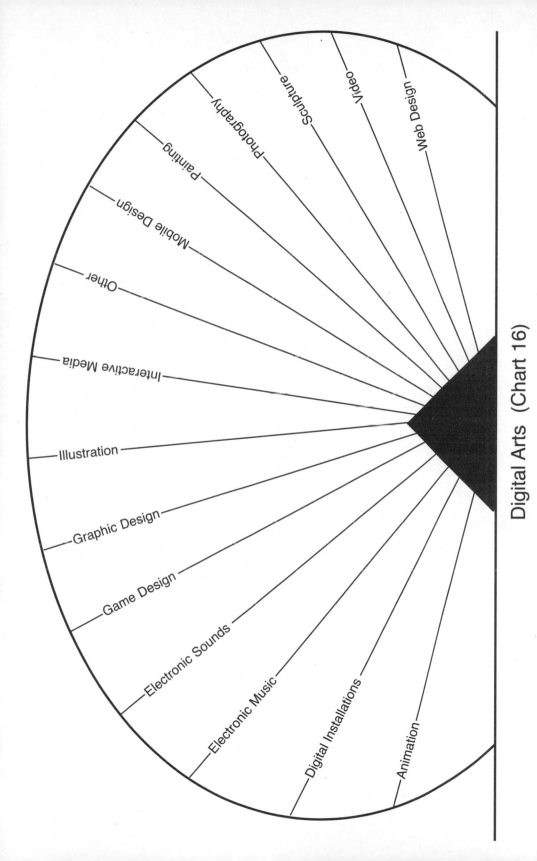

Digital Arts (Chart 16)

Web Design
Video
Sculpture
Photography
Painting
Mobile Design
Other
Interactive Media
Illustration
Graphic Design
Game Design
Electronic Sounds
Electronic Music
Digital Installations
Animation

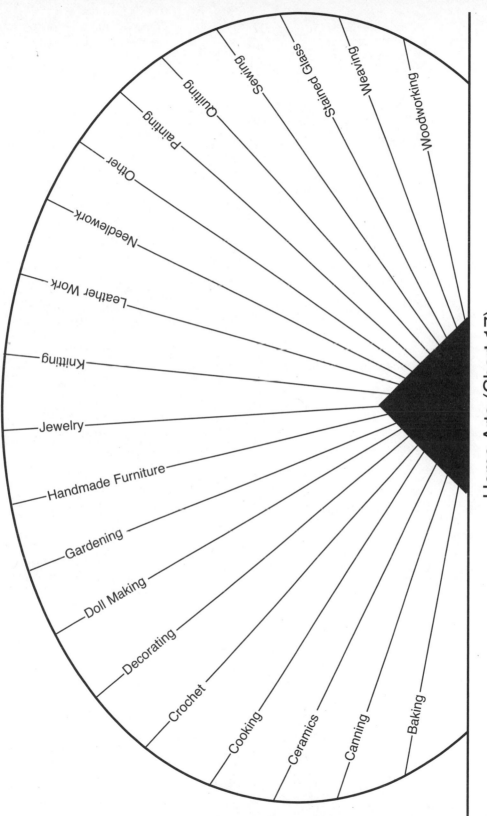

Home Arts (Chart 17)

Woodworking
Weaving
Stained Glass
Sewing
Quilting
Painting
Other
Needlework
Leather Work
Knitting
Jewelry
Handmade Furniture
Gardening
Doll Making
Decorating
Crochet
Cooking
Ceramics
Canning
Baking

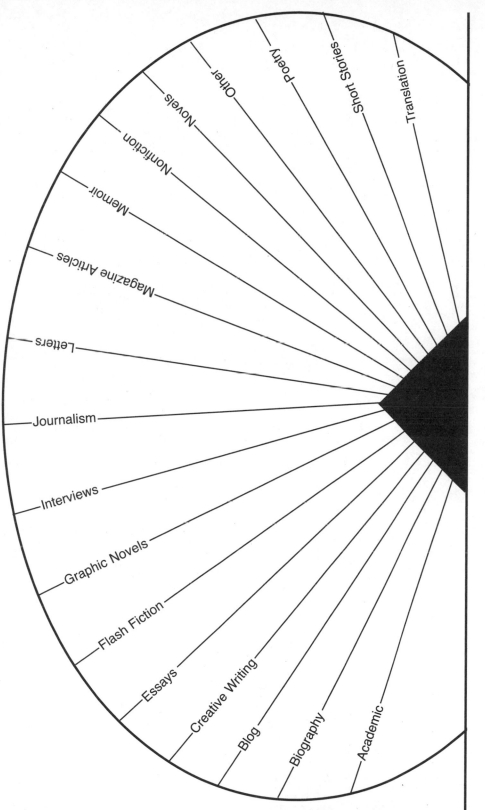

Literary Arts (Chart 18)

Translation
Short Stories
Poetry
Other
Novels
Nonfiction
Memoir
Magazine Articles
Letters
Journalism
Interviews
Graphic Novels
Flash Fiction
Essays
Creative Writing
Blog
Biography
Academic

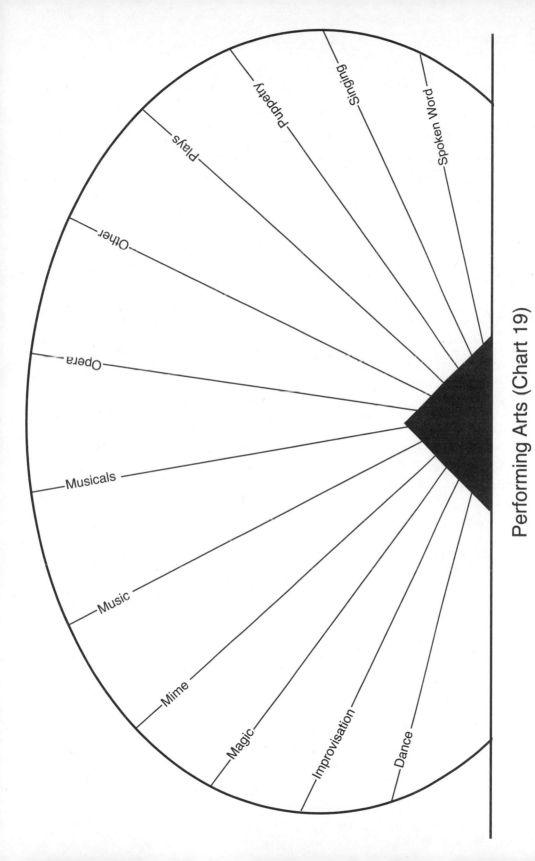

Performing Arts (Chart 19)

Spoken Word
Singing
Puppetry
Plays
Other
Opera
Musicals
Music
Mime
Magic
Improvisation
Dance

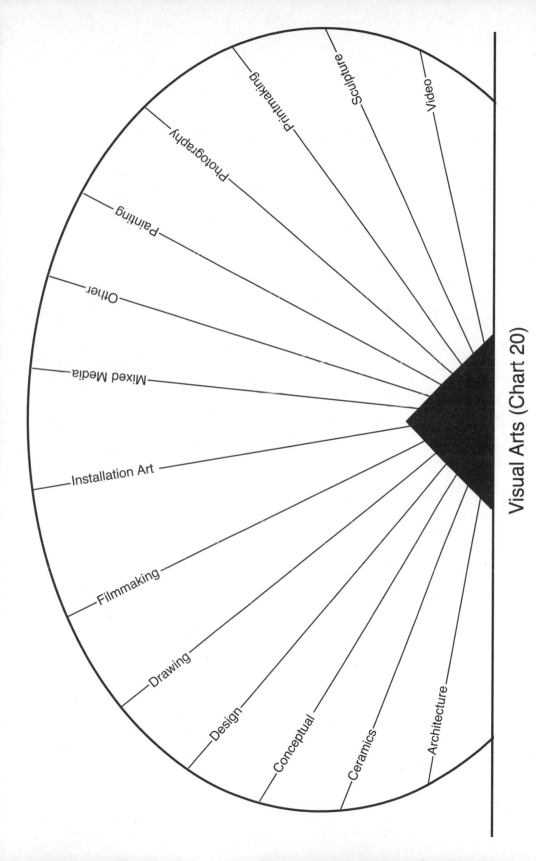

Visual Arts (Chart 20)

Video

Sculpture

Printmaking

Photography

Painting

Other

Mixed Media

Installation Art

Filmmaking

Drawing

Design

Conceptual

Ceramics

Architecture

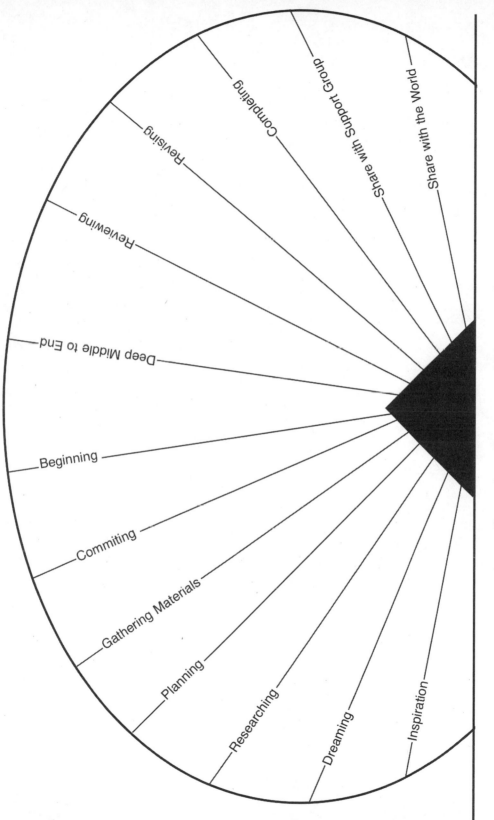

Creative Process (Chart 21)

Inspiration
Dreaming
Researching
Planning
Gathering Materials
Commiting
Beginning
Deep Middle to End
Reviewing
Revising
Completing
Share with Support Group
Share with the World

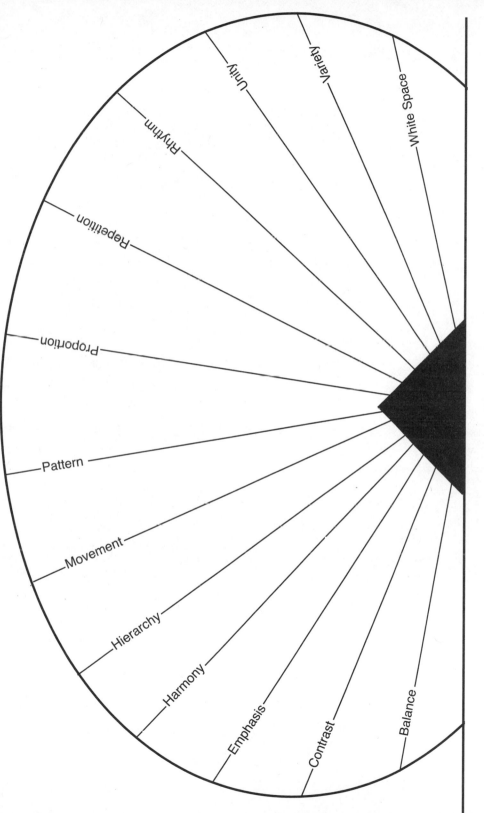

Principles of Design (Chart 22)

Variety

White Space

Unity

Rhythm

Repetition

Proportion

Pattern

Movement

Hierarchy

Harmony

Emphasis

Contrast

Balance

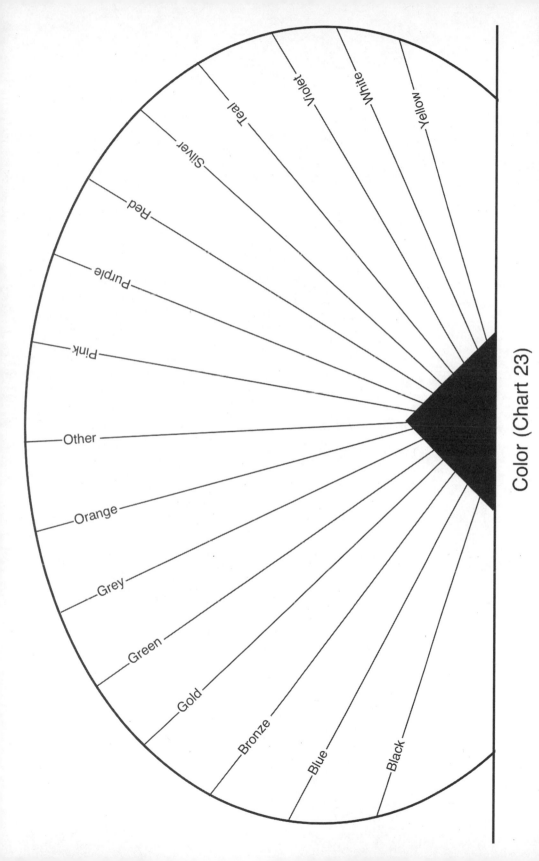

Color (Chart 23)

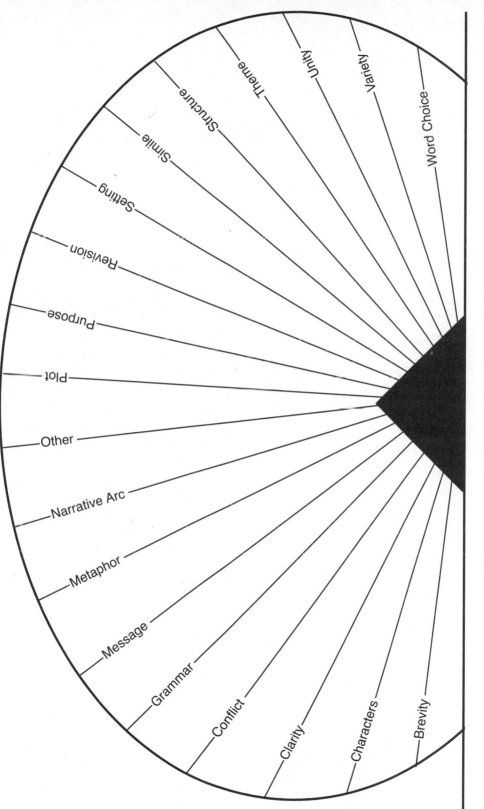

Elements of Story & Writing (Chart 24)

Word Choice
Variety
Unity
Theme
Structure
Simile
Setting
Revision
Purpose
Plot
Other
Narrative Arc
Metaphor
Message
Grammar
Conflict
Clarity
Characters
Brevity

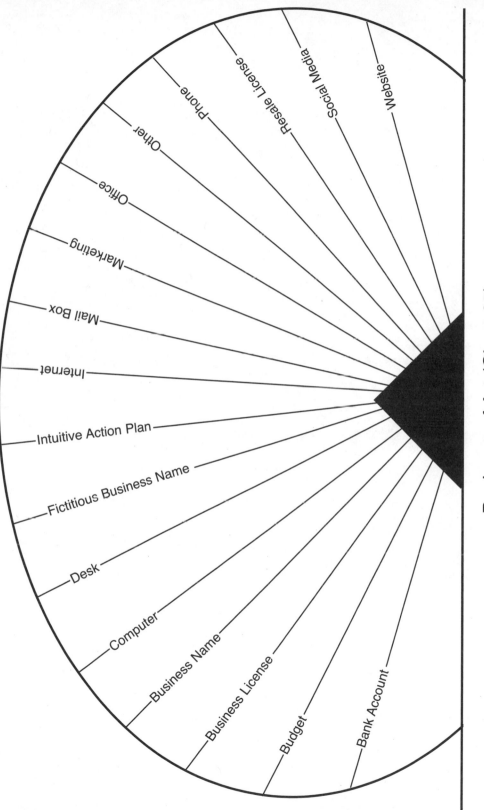

Business of Art (Chart 25)

Website
Social Media
Resale License
Phone
Other
Office
Marketing
Mail Box
Internet
Intuitive Action Plan
Fictitious Business Name
Desk
Computer
Business Name
Business License
Budget
Bank Account

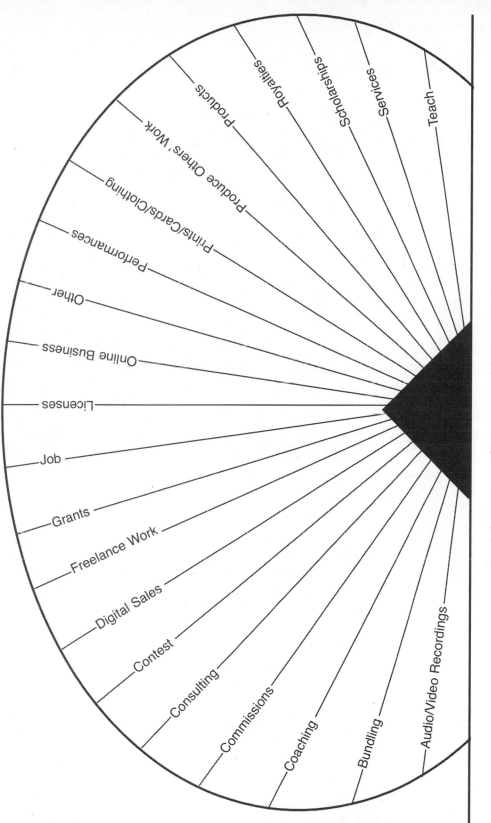

Income Streams (Chart 26)

Teach
Services
Scholarships
Royalties
Products
Produce Others' Work
Prints/Cards/Clothing
Performances
Other
Online Business
Licenses
Job
Grants
Freelance Work
Digital Sales
Contest
Consulting
Commissions
Coaching
Bundling
Audio/Video Recordings

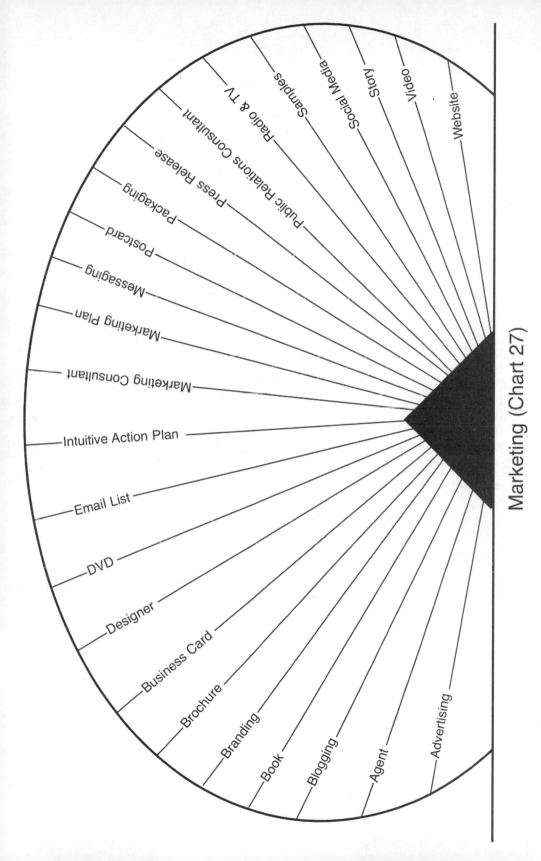

Marketing (Chart 27)

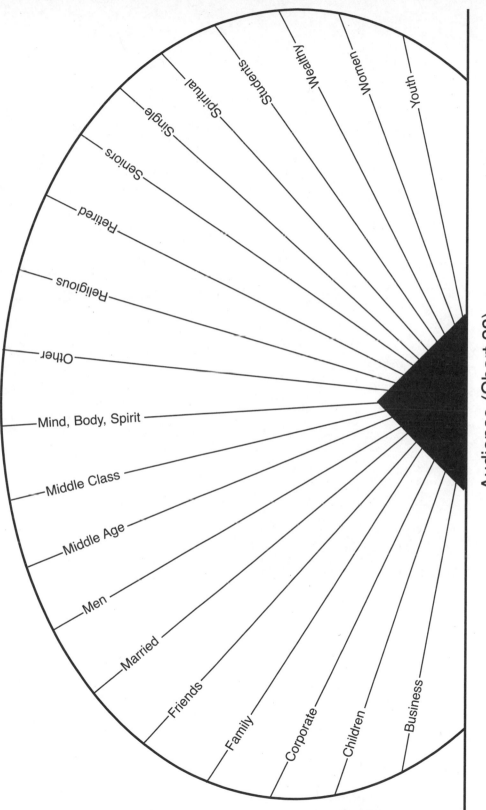

Audience (Chart 28)

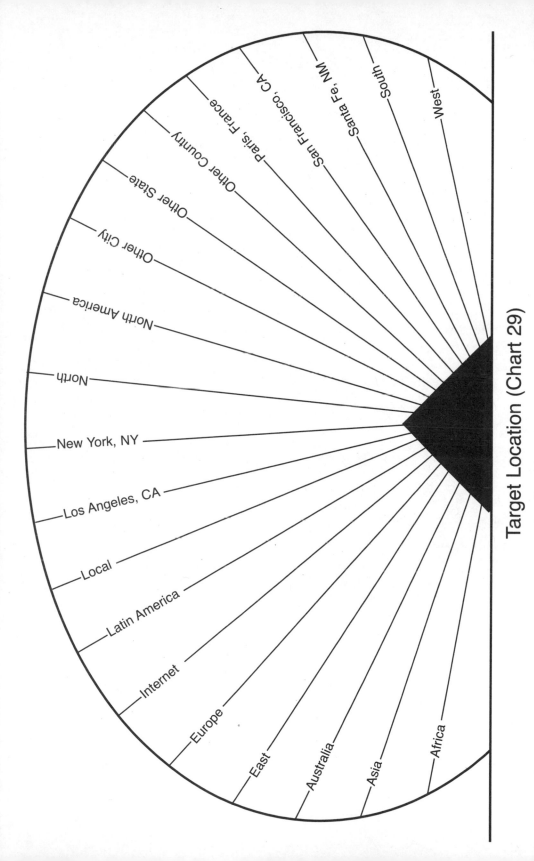

Target Location (Chart 29)

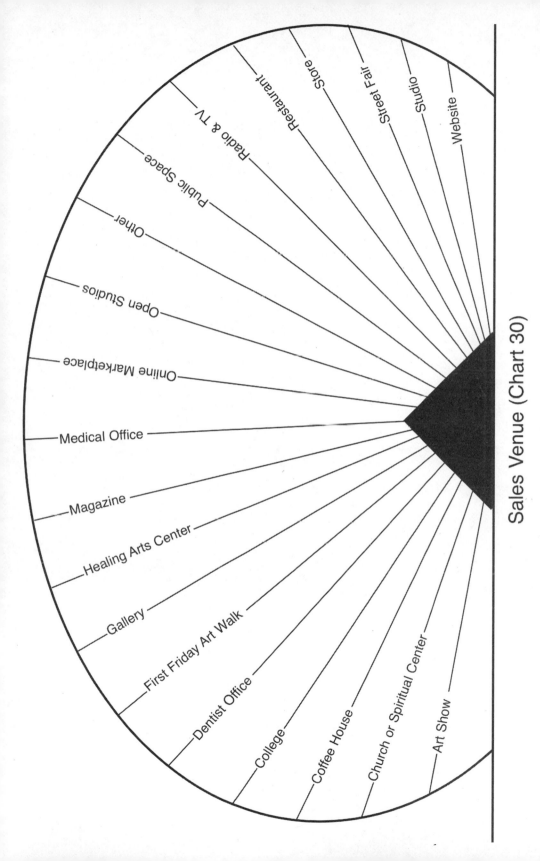

Sales Venue (Chart 30)

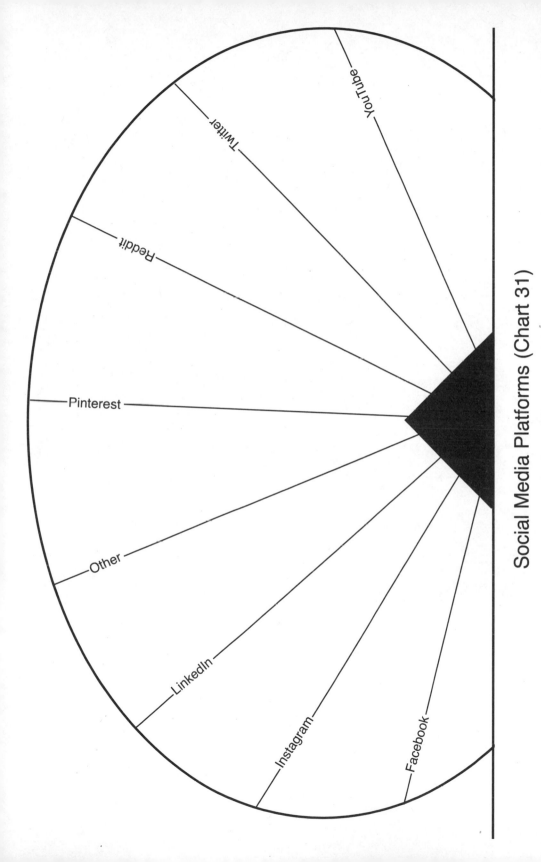

Social Media Platforms (Chart 31)

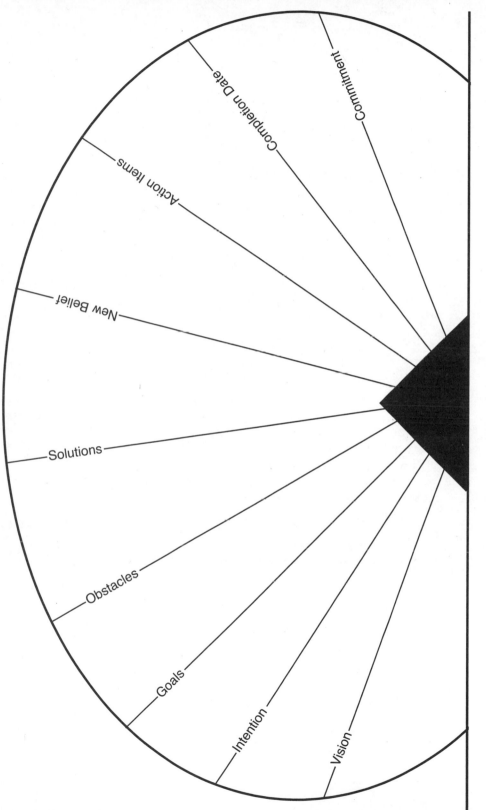

Intuitive Action Plan (Chart 32)

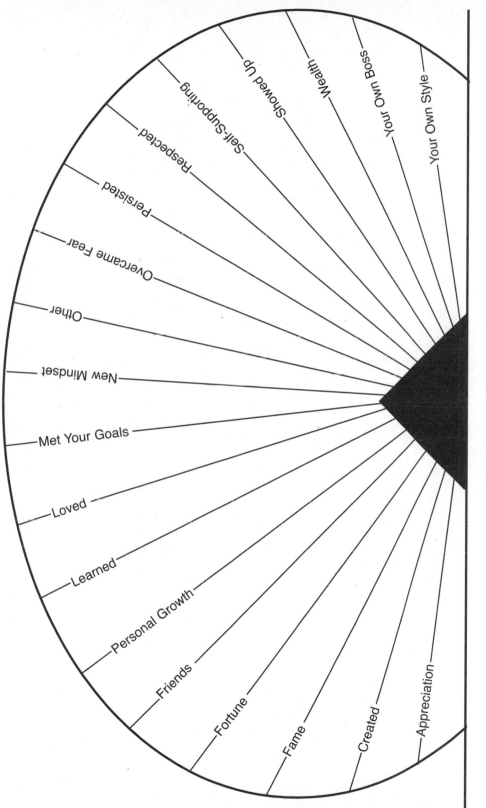

Success (Chart 33)

ABOUT THE AUTHOR

Joan Rose Staffen is a writer, artist, and psychic healer dedicated to assisting others to heal their lives, rediscover their purpose, and stay on their life path. On the spiritual path since her early twenties, she has explored many healing modalities including psychic healing, yoga, meditation, a Course in Miracles, Unity Church principles and prayers, and spiritual response therapy, a dowsing system for deep healing. Joan has facilitated Artist Way groups in Santa Cruz and Marin Counties, and has helped coach numerous budding and recovering artists.

Other Books by the Author

The Book of Pendulum Healing: Charting Your Healing Course for Mind, Body, and Spirit

Divination and Action: Intuitive Tools for an Inspired Worklife

Divination and Joy: Intuitive Tools for an Inspired Life

Swimming the Inner Ocean

Through Love

TO OUR READERS